Everyday Activities to Help Your Young Child with Autism Live Life to the Full

by the same author

Yoga for Children with Autism Spectrum Disorders
A Step-by-Step Guide for Parents and Caregivers
Dion E. Betts and Stacey W. Betts
Forewords by Louise Goldberg, Registered Yoga Teacher, and Joshua S. Betts
ISBN 978 1 84310 817 7

Hints and Tips for Helping Children with Autism Spectrum Disorders
Useful Strategies for Home, School, and the Community
Dion E. Betts and Nancy J. Patrick
ISBN 978 1 84310 896 2

Asperger Syndrome in the Inclusive Classroom
Advice and Strategies for Teachers
Stacey W. Betts, Dion E. Betts and Lisa N. Gerber-Eckard
Foreword by Peter Riffle
ISBN 978 1 84310 840 5

of related interest

Speech in Action
Interactive Activities Combining Speech Language Pathology and Adaptive Physical Education
America X Gonzalez, Lois Jean Brady and Jim Elliott
ISBN 978 1 84905 846 9

Social Communication Cues for Young Children with Autism Spectrum Disorders and Related Conditions
How to Give Great Greetings, Pay Cool Compliments and Have Fun with Friends
Tarin Varughese
ISBN 978 1 84905 870 4

Motivate to Communicate
300 Games and Activities for Your Child with Autism
Simone Griffin and Dianne Sandler
ISBN 978 1 84905 041 8

Get out, Explore, and Have Fun!
How Families of Children with Autism or Asperger Syndrome Can Get the Most out of Community Activities
Lisa Jo Rudy
ISBN 978 1 84905 809 4

Everyday Activities to Help Your Young Child with Autism Live Life to the Full

Simple Exercises to Boost Functional Skills, Sensory Processing, Coordination and Self-Care

Debra S. Jacobs
and Dion E. Betts

Foreword by
Carol A. Just, OTD, OTR/L

Jessica Kingsley *Publishers*
London and Philadelphia

Front cover image source: iStockphoto®. The cover image is for illustrative purposes only, and any person featuring is a model.

First published in 2012
by Jessica Kingsley Publishers
116 Pentonville Road
London N1 9JB, UK
and
400 Market Street, Suite 400
Philadelphia, PA 19106, USA

www.jkp.com

Library of Congress Cataloging in Publication Data
Jacobs, Debra S. (Debra Sue), 1959-
  Everyday activities to help your young child with autism live life to the
full : simple exercises to boost functional skills, sensory processing,
coordination, and self-care / Debra S. Jacobs and Dion E. Betts ; foreword by
Carol A. Just.
    p. cm.
  Includes bibliographical references and index.
  ISBN 978-1-84905-238-2 (alk. paper)
  1. Autism in children--Popular works. 2. Occupational therapy for children-
-Popular works. I. Betts, Dion E. (Dion Emile), 1963- II. Title.
  RJ506.A9J328 2012
  618.92'85882--dc23
                                    2011031922

British Library Cataloguing in Publication Data
A CIP catalogue record for this book is available from the British Library

ISBN 978 1 84905 238 2
eISBN 978 0 85700 482 6

Printed and bound in the United States

Contents

Foreword

Debra Jacobs and her co-author Dion Betts have developed an excellent resource for families who are struggling daily in their homes with challenges related to raising a child with an Autism Spectrum Disorder (ASD).

The most recent statistics from AutismSpeaks.com (2011), a website providing information on autism, estimates that one in every 110 children is diagnosed with autism. US Government statistics suggest the prevalence rate of autism is increasing 10 to 17 percent annually. It is not known why the incidence is increasing, but improved diagnostic tools and the environment may be contributing factors. Recent studies find boys are more likely than girls to develop autism and receive the diagnosis three to four times more frequently (AutismSpeaks.com 2011).

Individuals with ASDs are unique in their cluster of characteristics, but all demonstrate challenges in the area of delayed or disordered communication, restrictive or repetitive behaviors, and deficits in social communication. Most children with ASDs also exhibit sensory challenges that complicate daily activities such as bathing, dressing, and sleep (Kuhaneck and Watling 2010).

For example, children with ASDs may struggle with hypersensitive hearing. This can result in behavioral overreactions to common sounds such as the sound of their siblings chewing or the sound of a toilet flushing. Some children with ASDs experience severe touch sensitivity causing extreme meltdowns due to the touch of their clothes. Families often report these daily life challenges as the most difficult for the entire family.

This is a book to help the numerous families who are seeking clear, easy, and loving methods to help their children who are diagnosed with ASD. The thoughtful sensory strategies suggested here will help to regulate the child's sensory systems so daily life activities such as eating, getting dressed, and going to the grocery store can be successfully accomplished by the child and the family.

An occupational therapist is typically on the team, providing identification and intervention for a child with an ASD. The occupational therapist is the member of the team who has the knowledge base about the sensory processing issues in young children with ASDs. By listening carefully to each family's story, the occupational therapist can help provide insight into the sensory struggles of the young child. This book provides families with multiple strategies for promoting daily life activities through sensory adaptations to routines.

Our sensory systems are the primary receivers of all external, environmental information. The external sensory information joins the internal sensory information in the brain where it is integrated. The brain then makes a behavioral response based on all this information. The sensory systems are tactile, vestibular (movement), vision, smell, taste, auditory, and proprioception or information from our joints and muscles.

To put it simply, the brain integrates the information and selects the appropriate behavioral response for the situation, or it interprets the sensory information as a threat or an irritation and produces an inappropriate response. For those with an ASD, some external sensory information is perceived in the brain as a threat or irritation. This can cause an emotional/behavioral overreaction. A typical example is wearing clothes. Usually our bodies "feel" the touch of our clothes for a few seconds, then our brain suppresses the "feeling" of our clothes so we can focus on more important sensations at that moment.

The brain in an individual with an ASD may not suppress the "feeling" of clothes so the clothes cause a negative response because they irritate the body. Due to the constant awareness of the sensation of the clothes, the individual cannot focus on other meaningful environmental information including learning in school, listening to directions, and staying on task.

Dr A. Jean Ayres, a neuroscientist and an occupational therapist, developed these concepts of sensory processing. In the 1960s she reviewed all the current science on development and perception. As she studied children with learning issues, she created the first tests for identifying sensory issues. Research in sensory processing continues today, especially due to the increased incidence of ASDs.

The brain science behind sensory processing is complicated and ever changing due to new research every day. Debra Jacobs and Dion Betts took this complicated information and created an easy to understand and useful book to help families manage daily sensory frustrations for their children who experience sensory regulation issues. I applaud this book for promoting love, happiness, and function in families (see Kubler-Ross 1997; Lieberman and Scheer 2002; Zwaigenbaum *et al.* 2009).

Carol A. Just, OTD, OTR/L
Owner of Just Therapy Inc.
and Adjunct Faculty
Department of Occupational Therapy
Jefferson School of Health Professions
Thomas Jefferson University
Philadelphia, PA, USA

Acknowledgments

A special thanks to Nancy Stiller, PhD, The University of Arizona, for her editing, friendship, and wonderful laughter. I am very grateful for the many brilliant occupational therapists who have taught me so much and the profession of occupational therapy that encourages and nurtures creative expression and the fulfillment of potential in everyone.

To my co-author, thank you for leading me on this journey. A special thanks to Carol Just, OTD, OTR/L, for her enthusiasm from the start of this project, and her beautiful and informative foreword to this book. To the thousands of families I have worked with over the past 30 plus years, thank you for giving me the opportunity to fulfill my intention of healing the world one person at a time. Last, but not least, for the unconditional love and support from my amazing husband and wonderful children, Jim Jacobs and Brenda and Scott Tobin. Thank you. You three are my balance, my heart, and my soul.

Debra Jacobs

Joshua, Jacob, Daniel, Sarah, and Dora, my children, and my wife Stacey are a constant source of stimulation, fun, and ideas. My life and my contribution to this book would not have been possible without them. My co-author was the lead author and "idea machine" and I learned so much from her in our collaboration.

Dion Betts

A Note about This Book

It is important that parents, carers, and professionals seek a full occupational therapy assessment for children with developmental concerns. This book is not intended to replace the services of licensed occupational therapists. Rather, it is intended to supplement supports and services provided by such professionals. It is recommended that the advice of a qualified medical professional be sought prior to taking part in any physical regimen, such as those suggested in this book.

We have used male pronouns throughout this book for consistency and clarity of writing only. The suggestions here are as appropriate for girls with ASDs as they are for boys.

Introduction

What are Autism Spectrum Disorders?

Autism Spectrum Disorders (ASDs) fall under the diagnosis of Pervasive Developmental Disorder. Such disorders include Asperger Syndrome, autism, Childhood Degenerative Disorder, and Rhett Syndrome. These are not psychological disorders, but medical disorders which affect physical and social development. Brain chemicals, or neurochemicals, and their interactions in the brain are affected by these disorders. Research has not found the cause of ASDs, or indeed a cure.

Medications have been helpful in reducing some of the many symptoms of ASDs as have social skills therapies, speech therapy, physical therapy, occupational therapy, and others. Many more therapeutic approaches are being researched to assist in helping children develop physically and socially.

Occupational therapy has been used with great success in addressing symptoms and in enhancing the developmental processes of children with a variety of medical disorders and developmental disabilities. In many cases, people with ASDs have concurrent disorders relating to physical development. Additionally, siblings of children with ASDs have a disproportionately higher likelihood of also having an ASD.

Recent research shows early detection of ASDs in babies to be both challenging yet necessary. Parents often report recalling problems in their children when they were less than two years of age. Some of these problems observed were delayed speech and language development, lack of responsiveness or social connectedness behavior difficulties, and in sleeping and feeding (Zwaigenbaum *et al.* 2009).

There are many disorders involving physical development that have an impact on all children, any of which can acutely affect the development of children with ASDs. Often, occupational therapists are key members of treatment teams and provide direct service to children and adults. They also provide consultation to other members of treatment teams and parents.

The purpose of this book is to provide accessible and comprehensive information about occupational therapy techniques to assist parents, carers, professionals, and treatment teams. This book is a personal consultation guide. The reader may choose specific topics of interest or read the book from start to finish. We hope this book will become a reference to which the reader will return frequently.

What is occupational therapy?

Occupational therapy uses activities to enhance the quality of life for an individual. Children with ASDs typically exhibit some developmental delays related to physical skills, learning, and social development. The activities presented in these pages fit naturally into family life. Children with ASDs, family members, and others can also enjoy these suggestions. When anyone is active in a pursuit, the brain pays focused attention, and the opportunity for growth is enhanced.

Functional assessment

The ideas presented in this book address the physical, social, motor, and cognitive demands of each activity, social interaction, or environment. Children with ASDs may be slow to acquire daily living skills, for example. Each skill is therefore broken down to its component so that skill development may proceed in a natural and calm way at the child's individual pace.

Skill assessment

While some of the activities are presented with age guidelines, these are only suggestions. Skills are addressed according to the child's developmental sequence, and each child will progress through those steps no matter his age.

Sensory processing

In addition to the five senses (touch, taste, smell, hearing, and vision), there are also the senses of personal space, movement, knowing where one is in space, and the movement of the whole or parts of the body. Often children with ASDs misinterpret or simply miss the cues their bodies or the environment provides. Children with ASDs and some sensory processing disorders may also pay more attention than necessary to one cue (a shiny earring the teacher is wearing, for instance) and miss the important information being provided, such as the next assignment. A menu of "sensory diets" is provided in Chapters 4 and 7. Following these diets will allow the child to feel more comfortable in the world, and become active in his own self-control.

Visual/motor skills

Such skills enable the eyes and hands to work together in a coordinated way to interpret visual cues and to act on those cues. This is specifically important in reading and following written directions. Visual/motor skills are used, for example, when placing silverware on the table to set, doing a homework assignment, or when kicking a soccer ball.

Self-care skills

These skills are also known as "activities of daily living" or adaptive skills. These are the tasks that help us to care for our self and interact with the world around us. Learning these skills requires some special considerations for children with ASDs. In Chapters 5 and 6 specific challenges are addressed as well as solutions for making personal and community involvement pleasant. The goal is that the children with ASDs become as independent as possible.

How to use this book

It is important to note that the information in this book should be used in conjunction with the consultation of an occupational therapist. Children with ASDs benefit most from a team approach of parents, carers, and professionals. This is the ideal. It is also recommended that such a team meet regularly and communicate via email and other methods. Noted improvements in the development of children with ASDs typically occur with a consistent team approach. Parents, carers, and professionals often note with great satisfaction the reaching of milestones and benchmarks in the lives of these children.

Chapter 1

Body Awareness

Many of the skills presented in this chapter are ones we all develop, but we do not think about. These perceptions or senses are discussed in just about every chapter in this volume.

In this book we have attempted to divide the ideas presented in a way that is accessible for everyone. There is inevitably some overlap between the chapters as we discuss these ideas—the person is a whole being, not neatly separated into skills and abilities that are acquired in isolation. We hope you will take away an understanding of these ideas. We encourage you to celebrate the wonderful and complex person that a child with ASD is, and to believe in a bright future.

Perceptions, or ways in which to understand the world, are the result of movement and experience. Movement may be caused by others, may be involuntary—such as in a reflex—or may be voluntary—that is, thought out ahead of time. At times movements are done without thinking or planning, and at other times much thinking and even visualization happens before a movement is made. Often we move because we are not comfortable with where our body is in space. We may need to make a slight adjustment to maintain balance or to avoid invading the space of another person. We make these slight adjustments all day without thinking about it. If you have ever seen a time-lapsed movie of people sitting at a concert, you will notice how much everyone moves in their seats. People even burn calories in their sleep, in large part due to continued movement in bed.

One example of knowing where our body is in space that causes us to move is when we are sitting at the edge of a chair. We need to move back to have a more secure seat. This feeling and the responding movement is the result of our body giving us accurate messages. If a child does not receive these messages accurately, he may fall or seem to be clumsy. You may have even seen a child who seems to be in constant movement, touching or leaning on whatever furniture or people are the closest to him. He does this constant adjusting because he does not understand the physical world around him. He moves continually so he can find a space where he is comfortable.

Children with ASDs do not experience the world in the same way as typical children. They may not develop the body awareness and insights needed to understand their surroundings by information gained from the movement of their bodies. Perhaps the child did not have some of the movement experience that other children did and so did not develop the innate understanding gained from those experiences. We can help by encouraging movement experiences that will develop these innate understandings. Learning occurs through moving and responding. The responses that occur from the experiences you offer the child will help him to learn and understand how his body works. He will also gain a greater understanding about the world around him and how to move through his environment.

One of the activities that takes up most of a child's time is learning that he has a body, what the parts do, and how those parts move. Infants also learn at a very young age that they are separate from the rest of the world. The typically developing child does this naturally through play. A baby with an ASD may not engage in the play activities that develop these senses, and so he needs some assistance and encouragement.

It is very important for the baby to move into different positions during the day. Adapting his body to different places or adjusting his position and vision is the way these senses naturally develop. A baby with an ASD may be very quiet and content to spend a good part of his time awake in a solid car seat/carrier "entertaining" himself. It is important that the baby is moved out of the car seat once a location is reached. Although it is very convenient to lift the entire baby seat out of the car and put it in a grocery cart, this is not recommended for a baby who may have an ASD. Lifting the baby, even if it is only to put him down again into a stroller, has great benefits. It helps him to exercise his neck and eye muscles as he adjusts to the new position.

Adapting to the movement of being lifted helps to exercise the muscles in his neck that will eventually help him to keep his head up. "Head lag" is the backwards motion a baby makes whose head is not supported when lifted. All very young babies have this, and this is why it is very important to support a young baby at the back of his head when he is lifted. By the time a typical baby is three months old, his neck muscles should be strong enough to support his head when he is lifted by his middle. However, babies with an ASD often have head lag longer than their developmentally typical peers. This is a result of not looking around and exploring the environment when left alone. They have not had the opportunity to exercise their neck muscles. Therefore it is very important for parents and carers to provide as many opportunities as possible for the baby to see something new. These unique sights encourage the baby to look around and exercise naturally.

Additionally, if a baby is lifted out of the car in a baby seat, he is not visually alerted to the fact that something new is going on. His nervous system is not alerted. He continues to look in only one direction—forward. If he attempts to look to the side, he is met by the sides of the protective baby car seat. The view does not change. He has seen this pattern hundreds of times in his short life and it does not move or change and holds very little, if any, interest. It is as if he has blinders on.

A brief hug and the feeling of being held close as he is taken out of the car seat is wonderful and contributes to his sense of being. This point cannot be made strongly enough. But you may be thinking that "grocery shopping will be impossible if I do not use the car seat and keep the baby in the seat while I am shopping." Of course there will be times when keeping the baby in the seat is unavoidable. In those cases do so. Then, when all the groceries are stowed away, and the baby seat is once again strapped into the car, take the baby out. Hold him close for a few minutes, show him around the parking lot, and hold him alternatively close and far from your face.

These extra few minutes a day can make a great difference in his development, giving him exercise and a new opportunity to learn. The typical baby swing or bouncers are also great ways to provide and encourage movement in the very young child. The key thing to remember is to allow the baby or young child to experience a variety of movements throughout the day.

Another way to provide your very young infant movement opportunities is to give him the opportunity to lie on his stomach. The infant uses a lot of energy to hold his head up and so develops neck, shoulder, and upper body strength in a belly on the ground position. This is important for developing stability, so that when he is in a seated position, he will be able to use his hands and fingers without needing to move his entire arms.

Place a preferred blanket on the floor and get down there with the baby. Being face to face with the baby and allowing him to touch your face provides a great deal of learning opportunities. The baby will learn from this experience. At first he may touch your face or a toy spontaneously, as if by accident. As he gains more control over his movements, the baby will try to touch another person or a toy because this is something he enjoys. Perhaps he enjoys the happy sound you make when he touches your face. Perhaps he also enjoys the soft feel of the plush toy he has been able to reach. This purposeful reaching is a great milestone. The baby is learning that he can control his movements and he has an impact on the world around him.

Allow the baby time to acknowledge your presence and to look at you. This may take longer than you like. Take it slow. Be patient as you try to get the baby's attention. If you call his name, call it once, then wait. This waiting time may be as long as 30 seconds. This will allow the baby to understand that he heard your voice, it was directed at him, and it has some meaning. Once he gains this understanding, he will respond by looking at you. After he looks at you he may then reach for the toy or your face. If you continue to say his name over and over, without wait time, he needs to start the process of understanding regarding what he is hearing all over again. He may become frustrated and just not bother because he senses that there is too much being asked of him. He may also respond with frustration and become very upset. Remember to give the baby time, breathe deeply, and allow yourself to slow down.

When providing toys to a baby whom you may suspect has an ASD, be aware of the elements of the toy. Many toys have a variety of colors, textures, and produce sounds with the slightest touch. Be aware of the child's reactions to different toys. Many babies and children with ASDs are extremely sensitive to a variety of elements or information provided simultaneously. The baby's first toys should be black and white to provide a great visual contrast.

As you notice the baby enjoying this activity, see if adding a toy with a similar color scheme and a sound, such as a rattle, changes the baby's reaction. If he becomes upset by the rattle sound, this may mean that he is getting too much information at once. Remove the rattle and allow him to play with the more silent toys. He may enjoy the rattle as he gets a bit older.

Use this same technique for the texture of toys. Many baby toys are soft and plush, others are smooth and hard, and others still may have a variety of textures. Pay careful attention to the textures that the baby appears to enjoy the most. These will be the ones he reaches for, holds, and puts into his mouth. Remember, the greater the variety the baby has to experience, the more information he will be getting from the environment. The more information he is exposed to, the more he is learning. That learning comes in the form of understanding that he is separate from the world around him. However, there is a delicate balance between providing too much for the child and just enough so that he learns and is challenged. Keep in mind that what may be interesting and a great learning opportunity one day may be boring or too much the next. Like typical children, children with ASDs will have good days and bad, and develop likes and dislikes based on personal preferences.

You are the expert with your child and know him best. If you see that the child is getting upset with a certain toy, texture, or sound, remove it. He may feel more comfortable with this stimulation later on. When a baby, or anyone, no matter the age, feels stressed, learning does not take place. If the baby or child is upset by something, he is not open to the learning opportunity presented. His system is concerned with the negative response to whatever it is that is upsetting.

As humans, we have some very basic survival mechanisms that take over when we are upset. If something is stressful, our overall system goes into survival mode. If we are in this survival mode, then our muscles get tight, and our breathing and blood pressure rises. "Fight or flight" refers to a reaction to fear or stress. Adrenaline kicks in, and generally, anger or the desire to flee becomes present.

Think of the baby who is crying, clenching his fists as he bends his arms and legs, while his face is turning red. Any casual observer will know that this child is in distress. No new learning will occur when this is going on. Children with ASDs may not have a full-blown distress scene every time they are upset, but they may have some signs. One clear example may be that even if their entire face is not turning red, their ears may be. This is true for babies and for older children.

If the child is experiencing something that is upsetting, he may not move away, but his ears, especially the tops of his ears, may be turning red. Children with ASDs may not have the words to communicate that they are upset. At this point being an advocate for the child can be wonderful on a number of levels. You may say something like, "If you are scared to go into the movie theater, it's okay. We don't have to go inside." This can have a great impact on the child. First you are communicating to him that you are aware of the fact that he is upset. Then you are providing him with a possible reason for his feeling upset and helping him to take action, "deciding not to go in."

This sort of modeling can help empower the child and show him that there are solutions to things that upset him. By helping the child through this process, you are helping him to increase his self-awareness, demonstrating appropriate behavior. In later chapters we will discuss other methods to help the child learn to calm himself during stressful, difficult, and challenging times.

Exploring the different ways children learn can be an exciting and interesting adventure. Occupational therapists use a "multi-sensory" approach. That is, the occupational therapist often presents the same information in a variety of ways to determine what is interesting to the child, and how the information can be presented so that the child understands it. The variety of ways that information may be presented includes through movement, sound, or visually.

Touch may be very effective to increase body awareness in a very young child. Holding a baby with a firm pressure not only feels wonderful for the person holding the baby, but also provides information to the baby's nervous system that he "exists." Some children prefer a strong touch while others only enjoy or tolerate a light gentle touch. You know the child best and can determine his specific preferences. These suggestions are general, and can and should be adapted for the individual child.

Bath time is a great time to provide that extra information the baby or child needs about body awareness. Tell the child the name of the part as each part of the body is soaped and rinsed. You may add more information for older children. For example, tell the child, "This is your *right* hand for picking up toys and holding your spoon." It is never too early to start this process. Children with ASDs learn with repetition. Do not be surprised one day when your child names the body parts he has learned.

After a bath, as long as the child is young enough to bathe with help, use a large towel and wrap him up. Providing a snug wrap while rubbing firmly provides wonderful information about where his body starts and stops. This is a great daily way to provide some needed information to children with ASDs. Often these children have a low sense of where their body is in space and need that extra information to develop personal boundaries. This sense of personal space and position is something we do not think about, but allows us to know where we are and the position our body is in without looking. This snug wrap and firm rub is also very relaxing and a good idea to include in the night time bedtime routine.

If you notice that the child greatly enjoys the snug wrap of the towel, this feeling can continue after the bath. There are even specifically designed clothes that provide this sort of feeling. This clothing is not tight, but does provide some compression. Some styles look like super heroes or princesses, while others are simple colors. This sort of "sensory sensitive" design is becoming more and more popular and readily and commercially available. You may discover that the child will be relaxed and emotionally "available" to you when he feels more comfortable in his own body.

Firm rubbing is a good way to alert the senses of the child. Much of the information we get is from the skin. There are many opportunities for this activity that fit into the daily family routine. Although the purpose of this book is not to have the family become "therapists" and have specific therapy sessions at home, the goal is to provide therapeutic opportunities for the family to engage in during the course of the typical day.

Using lotion after a bath or sunscreen before going to play outdoors is another time when some firm rubbing can be provided to the child. Notice how the child reacts to this sort of touch. If he seems to enjoy it, then you have found something that can create a common bond. The goal is for children with ASDs to learn what they need to be comfortable. After learning their specific needs, they can learn to address them for themselves as another step towards independence. If the child does not enjoy the touch you are providing, then change it. The child will let you know by the way he responds if you are being too strong or too gentle with your touch. Experiment with different pressures when applying lotion until you find one that is enjoyable to the child.

The child may also like touch in some parts of his body and not others. For example, the back is a very popular spot for some nice deep rubs, but the bottoms of the feet may not elicit the same response. Showing the child that you are willing to find something he enjoys communicates a great deal of love. Don't be surprised to find the child bringing you the lotion other than at bath time. This is his way of communicating that he wants the touch or perhaps even the scent of the lotion. Rejoice in this successful communication with the child! You have reached the child through touch and he is reaching out to you. More communication may be built on this strong foundation.

As the child develops, activities that involve craft supplies and tool use similar to the ones used in school can be helpful in developing body awareness. Using the same supplies used at school can also help with skill development and school success as the child becomes competent in his use at home. Here is one example of a craft project that can increase body awareness in the school-age child.

Let's make a paper me

Table-top activities use fine motor skills and develop sequencing and tool use. This craft activity can be done in a number of sessions.

1. Have the child put his hand down flat on a piece of paper with his fingers spread wide.

2. Trace his hand (or have the child do the tracing if he is able, with a contrasting color). While tracing, bump each web space between each finger to give that added touch input. Help the child to keep one hand (non-dominant if it is known) down on a piece of paper while tracing with the other hand. Enjoy the gasp of delight as the child lifts his hand from the paper and sees the outline of his hand. Tell the child, "This is your hand."

3. Cut out the hand outline. This is also an excellent way to develop bilateral hand skills. This can be repeated on the other side and saved to make a "whole person" later on.

4. Have the child lie down on the floor and trace around his body. If the child is able to tell you the parts he wants to trace next, that would be great. Touch the part of the body that is the focus of the tracing.

5. Have the child color, or otherwise decorate the paper parts, until you have a complete outline, in life size.

6. Display this "Paper Me" and refer to it during body parts learning. If the child has something that hurts, this is a great way to help him communicate with you about what is going on in his body.

Often the child enjoys when adults have a turn. Place your hand down on a piece of paper so that he may trace the outline of your fingers. He may just scribble on the paper, and trace one or two fingers at a time. Allow him to proceed at his own pace, whether it is your hand or his own that he is tracing. After he completes the tracing of your five fingers, lift your hand so he can see what he has accomplished.

Share your enthusiasm by showing him that he has successfully traced your hand by lifting it up and down on the outline. Encourage him to do the same with the outline of his hand. Encourage him by simply pointing first to his hand and then to the paper. Allow him time, perhaps 30 seconds or more, before he responds. This repetitive behavior is teaching him that he can trace his hand and his marks on paper have meaning. Then he is learning that he can repeat this hand lifting to see what he has done. This increases his awareness of his own hand.

Being aware of and looking at the same thing as another person is called "joint attention." Joint attention is a behavior that is commonly lacking or delayed in children with an ASD. Sharing a moment as described above allows the child to experience joint attention. Increasing these experiences allows the child to increase his communication skills and his awareness of himself and others. Although it is tempting to look at the paper with the child, do your best to look at his face. He may for just a moment look at you, and you do not want to miss that precious eye-to-eye connection.

Another fun way to help the child develop self-awareness is with the use of a mirror. Allow the child to look into a mirror. Get behind him so that he may view you as well. Remove yourself from the image in the mirror so that only the child is in view. Repeat this, so the child pays attention to the different views in the mirror. A typically developing child will most likely talk to himself in the mirror and reach out to touch the image. Children with ASDs may treat the mirror image as any other image. They may move their arms or touch their faces while they are looking at the image. By doing so, you are adding touch and movement to the visual image. Now the child has multiple ways to understand the image in the mirror.

Using a routine activity is another way to increase the child's understanding of his image. Seat him in front of the mirror as you brush his hair or teeth. He is seeing what is happening to the image in the mirror as he feels his own hair and teeth being touched. This can be done with dressing, face painting, or any other activity that involves daily care or fun activities.

Right/left discrimination and self and others in the environment

Knowing which side is right and which is left is important in demonstrating to the world and to oneself that the child knows where he is and how the world is organized. Right and left discrimination can be divided into three parts. They are the right and left side of oneself, other individuals, and objects in the world. The world we live in, for the most part, is set up for people with a right dominant hand. Many children with ASDs have a delay in determining if they are right or left handed. When this is finally decided, many more than average turn out to have a left dominant hand. This further makes life complicated for these children.

Here are a few daily activities you can do to provide the child with learning tools, so he can begin to understand the world a little better from a right and left-sided approach. When a child really knows right and left, he doesn't have to think about it. The child will respond automatically when given a direction. When a child is stressed or unsure about right and left, he needs to concentrate more than when he is relaxed.

Many childhood songs use body movements, especially right and left. These are great learning tools. You may notice that children with

ASDs greatly enjoy music. Take advantage of this interest to teach skills. Even if you are not using a specific song at the time, the child may pay attention to you if you state your information in a sing-song voice. Try it and you may be pleasantly surprised.

Unless it is a round shape, like a ball, you can distinguish the right and left sides of just about any object in the environment. Take learning opportunities as they present themselves daily. Use the child's favorite objects to further his knowledge. Point out to him the elements the objects contain, such as sides, shapes, textures, and colors. For example, if you are looking at a book with the child, point out that his favorite character is pictured on the right or left side of the page. Doing this a few times a day in a variety of settings and situations will increase the child's awareness that objects have a right and left side.

My right hand

The first step in understanding the world in terms of right and left sides is for the child to understand that he has a right and left side.

1. During bath time, identify the right and left side of the body as washing progresses. "These are your right toes..." and so on.

2. When getting dressed, ask the child to stick out his right foot, so you can put the sock on his right foot. If he is incorrect or uncertain, wait for a reply. After 10 to 15 seconds hold his right foot, and as you place the sock on say, "This is your right foot." Continue this activity with other articles of clothing. If time is too short to wait for the child to respond after each item of clothing, then do it at least once. Use different body parts and articles of clothing each time. Doing this daily will give the child the idea that in fact he does have a right and left side to his body.

3. When walking and holding the child's hand, tell him which hand you are holding. This gives him the idea that all day long these sides of the body remain the same. Swinging the child's arm as you walk along reinforces the awareness of the arm with movement.

4.   When the child is eating or drinking, talk to him about what he is doing. Bring his attention to the fact by saying, "You are holding your cup in your left hand."

5.   Some children have a favorite bracelet or watch that they wear every day. Usually this will be worn on the same wrist. This is a great opportunity to identify his right or left side. This may also be used as a cue for him in school.

6.   Many childhood songs celebrate the right and left sides of the body, such as "The Hokey Pokey." Dancing and singing are great ways to learn. The mind is alerted to the information when it is presented in a rhythmic and melodious fashion.

Mom's right hand

The second step in understanding that there are two sides is gaining awareness that other people have two distinct sides as well. Children with ASDs have a difficult time seeing things from another's perspective. This is a good way to bring their attention to the idea that others have sides also. Those sides may not be the same as the child's. This is best shown when facing a child and his right hand is in front of your left hand.

Most adults wear a watch on their left hand. Explaining this to the child and with repetition over time will teach him that Mom or Dad wears a watch on the left wrist. There are many opportunities to alert the child to the right and left sides of others. For example, if someone the child sees on a regular basis comes to visit you can say something like, "Say hello to Grandma Sophie. She wears her blue ring on her right hand." Shaking hands or song games that include hand shaking are a great way to demonstrate that other individuals have a right and left side too.

The bed has a right and left side

Becoming aware of the sides of objects in the environment is the most complex level of understanding right and left sides. We do not think about the fact that most on/off buttons are placed on the right side of objects. We take it for granted that when presented with written materials, we open a book from the right side and read from left to right. Spend a few minutes each day looking at objects in the environment with the child. Wonder out loud about obvious characteristics and of the right and left sides of what you see. Here are some ideas to reinforce the concept of right and left without using verbal language.

1. When reading to the child, have him sit on your lap or next to you so that he can see the words and pictures in the book.

2. Hold his index finger (use his dominant hand if you are sure which one it is; otherwise use his right finger).

3. Move his finger along the words as you read the text. You do not need to do this for the entire story if the child is expressing discomfort with you moving his finger. However, do continue to do this each time you start reading. The child will gradually enjoy this and may even lift your finger himself to move it along as a way to show you that he wants to be read to.

4. Ask the child to point out parts of the picture with the right or left directions included. For example, you can ask, "What color hat is the bear on the right side wearing?"

5. As the child learns right and left, you can increase the challenge by adding top/bottom and middle to the daily games.

6. Have the child help set the table in a specific way. Provide a model and allow him to add only one piece at a time. For example, put the fork on the left.

Balance

Learning to walk is a natural accomplishment as the child develops the skills to maintain his balance in an upright position on two legs. Developing good balance is an important part of feeling right in the world. Balance is not only accomplished by the muscles of the body; leg muscles are also important. The strength of the core muscles or the stomach and back muscles are just as important as the leg muscles for balance.

The mind and the eyes also play a big role in developing balance skills. When a child is walking, he is actually planning ahead each step and watching where he is headed. Adjustments need to be made if the ground is hard or soft, wet, dry, or slippery. Even more adjustments need to be made if the surface is uneven, such as on a hike outdoors or if there are stairs to climb. This planning takes place automatically in a typical child as he works against gravity to learn to walk.

Many children with ASDs have some difficulty with balance. They may trip, fall, or avoid climbing play activities. We can help children with ASDs develop these skills now that we understand how balance is developed. When the child has good balance, he has a greater sense of confidence overall. Standing and seated balance are important skills to develop.

When a child is able to stand or sit still, he is demonstrating good balance. If he continues to need to adjust his body, this shows that he is not comfortable and is working to "get his balance." Imagine if you were always walking on a slick icy road or a bumpy one with smooth leather shoes. You would be expending a lot of energy and extra movements to keep yourself upright.

Successful bicycle riding is the end result of good balance. To ride a two-wheeler, a child must be able to sit up straight, hold the handlebars, and peddle. While he is doing this, his back and stomach muscles are keeping him in an upright position, while he is watching where he is going and determining the direction to steer. Even if he is headed in a straight line, there are subtle changes that need to be made to keep the bicycle headed in the proper direction. A certain amount of speed is also necessary to maintain momentum. Try these fun games that target the skills needed for bicycle riding.

Building bicycle skills

1. Have the child lay on his back with his feet in the air. By lying on his back, the child is getting a lot of support and only needs to concentrate on moving his feet.

2. The child will naturally bend his legs at the hip and the knee. Firmly grasp the child's feet. Gently pull one leg straight while bending the other leg.

3. Continue bending one leg while straightening the other in a smooth, slow, and rhythmic way.

4. Call this "Bicycle Legs" or any other name that has meaning to you and the child.

5. Once the child is comfortable with the movement, allow him to continue on his own. As he is able to move his legs, bending and straightening in an alternating way, it is time for the next step.

6. If a willing sibling or friend is available, have them both lie on their backs with the bottoms of their feet touching and move their legs as though they were riding a bicycle. The children are both on their backs with their heads facing in the opposite direction from each other.

7. A tricycle allows the child to gain the alternating or reciprocal movement skill needed to ride. The child does not need to do the extra work of keeping it upright. Gently push the tricycle from behind as the child's feet rest on the pedals. This will give the child a sense of the movement even if he is not causing it. It will encourage him to pedal independently.

8. The tricycle still requires that the child maintain an upright posture while seated. Some tricycles are available with a seat back for added support. By all means use this if the child needs it. It is beneficial for the child to experience the feeling of movement and the alternating pattern of his leg movement. The empowerment a child feels as he propels forward cannot be underestimated!

9. After the child masters the tricycle, it is time to move up to the two-wheeled bicycle with training wheels. The other exercises below that develop core strength will have a benefit for the skill of bicycle riding as well.

Another reason that children with ASDs may have difficulty with balance is because of diminished understanding of feedback from touch or movement. We will discuss these issues in later chapters.

Here are some fun games you can try with the child to help him to develop his balance skills.

Pillow walk

This "game" will encourage the natural balance reaction. It works on the planning skills that are an important part of good balance and visual awareness. To enhance imagination, make up a story about how the floor is a lake and you do not want to get wet. Get as imaginative as you like, using references from recent books you have read with the child or his favorite stories.

1. Place some pillows or cushions on the floor in a line or a circle. It is a good idea if the pillows have different amounts of stuffing. This will provide an opportunity to adjust to different feelings as the game progresses.

2. Show the child how you can walk on the pillows only, without your feet touching the floor. Showing your child how to "play" this game is the best way to communicate the instructions.

3. Start by walking in a straight line, then a circle, and finally a figure of eight pattern.

4. Support the child at first by holding his hand as he steps on the pillow.

5. This may be as far as you go for the first try. Step on, stand, and step off. Go at the child's pace. Always pay attention to the stress level of the child. Learning takes place when the child is relaxed and having fun, not when he is stressed.

6. Allow the child to take off his shoes as this will allow his feet to experience a lot of the touch sensation from the different textures of the materials covering the pillows.

Target practice

In this game, a challenge to balance is combined with some visual skills.

1. Have the child stand on a pillow. If he is unable to stand on a pillow, then standing on the floor works as well.

2. Place a trash can or large bowl in front of the child.

3.   Place this target close enough so that the child has a good chance of hitting the target.

4.   Using bean bags, small stuffed toys, or balls, throw the items into the bowl.

5.   As the child's skill develops, increase the challenge. Move the target further away from where he is standing, or raise it up so that it is off the floor.

6.   To increase the challenge to balance, have the child stand on two cushions. Balance can also be challenged by having the child stand on one foot, while throwing towards the target.

Up on your knees please

Tall kneeling or knee sitting is a very good position for strengthening back and stomach muscles (core) and improving balance.

1.   On the floor, fold your legs under while maintaining an upright position. Being a model is a great teaching tool.

2.   Assist the child as he gets into position.

3.   Make sure not to fold your legs in half by having the backs of your lower legs touching the backs of your thighs. Sit up tall with the front part of the bottom half of your legs only on the floor.

4.   It may be difficult to hold this position for more than a minute or even a few seconds at first. Allow a "rest" break by folding legs in half so the upper thighs rest on the backs of the calves (children will do this naturally, as it is an easier position to sit in) and then encourage the child to get up again for a longer period of time.

5.   Singing a song while in this position is a good way to help the time pass, and the exercise is doing its good work for the muscles and balance. The distraction of the song encourages more time in the exercise position.

6.   As the child becomes more comfortable in this position, he can hold it for longer periods of time and the adult does not need to model it.

7. Have the child sit in this position as a story is being read.

8. To add another challenge, play catch with the child as he maintains this tall kneeling upright position.

Mobility

Walking is the natural result of the development of the muscles and their victory over gravity. Children with ASDs may appear different when they walk. Their arms may move in a manner that seems to have nothing at all to do with the rhythm of their steps. They may take very small steps or their legs may be far apart as they walk. Perhaps the child's knees are not bending and he has trouble walking in a straight line. This awkward gait may be the result of poor balance, weak core muscles, or the need to understand where he is in space and how he is moving. No matter the reason, it is a good idea for the child to develop a smooth and balanced walking pattern.

To encourage a reciprocal gait pattern, demonstrate an exaggerated arm swing as you walk. Swing the right arm forward as the left leg steps forward, and so on.

Lifting the legs high as in a marching step will encourage knee and hip flexibility. Singing a song with a strong rhythm or making believe that you are in a marching band or a parade will encourage this walk.

Making sure the child's shoes are comfortable and secure is important. If the child is not wearing shoes that fit correctly or feel as though they are slipping off, this will distract the child as he is walking. He may subconsciously be spending a lot of time and energy keeping his shoes on his feet.

Getting to know children with ASDs is a challenging and rich journey. Celebrating the awareness and encouraging the child as he gets to know himself may be one of the most rewarding experiences of life.

Chapter 2

Increasing Coordination

Coordination consists of using different areas of the body together so that something meaningful is achieved. In this chapter we are going to talk about using the eyes and hands together to play and do other things with ease. Having good coordination allows for skill development with movement and tool use.

Eye–hand coordination

Showing the child an example along with spoken directions and reminders helps children with ASDs to better understand each activity described below. But use as few words as possible to describe what you are doing, and show more than talk about the activity. The child is more likely to understand physical instructions and can imitate actions rather than comprehend verbal directions. This may be true even if the child has an advanced vocabulary and appears to understand what is being said—for example, by nodding his head.

Eye–hand coordination is one of the first skills that a child develops. This is considered a visual motor skill. When a typically developing child holds his hand up in front of his face, he is learning "showing" himself his hand and how it moves. Then, as he gets a little older and begins to pick up toys, he will make the toys move or rattle and show himself that he can do this. At first learning is incidental and then intentional interaction with the environment allows for eye–hand coordination to develop naturally through play. Children with ASDs will often not "show" themselves their hands or their toys.

We must therefore be creative in encouraging the same development, but with some help. The goal of these activities is to have the child look at a moving object. The object will be moving because the child makes it move, and he is going to follow that object with his eyes. As they get older it is important that children with

ASDs use objects for their intended purpose and demonstrate an understanding of that purpose.

Infants: Birth to two years of age

Gain the child's attention by sound (calling his name or another sound he will pay attention to). Put an object with high contrast into his line of sight and provide a positive reward as soon as he glances at the object. Black and white toys provide good contrast; soft pastel colors do not. The reward could be a soothing "good job" or movement or touch that you know your baby enjoys. Then place the object in his hand. It is helpful if there is a soft elastic band attached to the toy, so the child has the experience of "holding" the object independently. This active participation is important for early feelings of control and independence, and awareness of having an impact in the world outside of him.

Continue to move the object as the child follows it with his eyes. Allow the child to move the object that is now gently attached to his wrist. When the child does not appear to be looking at the object, remove it from his wrist and begin the sequence again. Repeat this five times, three to four times throughout the day. As the child begins to look at objects that he is holding, he will no longer need the elastic strap attachment. Make sure to use at least three different toys for variety.

Toddlers: Ages two to five

Again it is important for the child to look actively in the direction of the object you want him to follow with his eyes. In a typically developing child, the accidental touch of an object is noted by a movement— either an attempt at a grasp or a push. The child demonstrates an awareness of the environment by acknowledging that he touched something. This acknowledgment may be in the form of a delighted noise or the attempt to move or touch the object again. As the child gets older, he will purposely use objects. He may imitate Dad shaving or brushing his hair, for example.

The child begins to understand that objects in the world are to be used and the child has the power to use them. Children with ASDs do not necessarily demonstrate that they are aware of touching an object and therefore do not practice the fine motor hand skills needed to manipulate that object in the environment. As the child gets older he will continue to have a delay in his eye–hand coordination because he is not actively seeking toys or other objects to use in a meaningful way. This lack of hand use to manipulate objects results in fine motor delays as the child continues to use his hands in only one way and not with a variety of movements.

A game that will encourage the child to use his hands in a variety of ways is to collect various objects and place them in a cloth bag or a pillowcase. Make sure the objects have different textures and shapes. Show the child the objects as you place them into the bag and name each one. Make sure that the object is within the line of sight of the child as it is placed in the bag. Have the child reach into the bag and pull out one object. He may need some physical assistance initially to get the idea of reaching in and pulling out. Once he has the object, have him show the object to you, and show it to him. While this is happening, verbalize each step of the way, and show him how to manipulate the object he has pulled out. Allow the child then to move and touch the object independently.

Examples of age-appropriate objects may be a ball, a small slinky, a set of keys, a spoon, a windup toy, or a small stuffed animal. This game will encourage the child to visualize items in his mind and develop the skill of object permanence (understanding that things continue to exist even when they are no longer seen). In addition, manipulating a variety of objects uses and strengthens different muscles of the hand. Try to avoid toys that require batteries or that react when a button is pushed. The goal is to have the child have an impact in the world, not press a button for results.

Swinging is a great activity for many skills. In this case, the child moves as he looks at the world. This movement is great exercise for the eyes, as the child is continually required to refocus his visual attention.

Children: Elementary school age

By now the typically developing child will have established a dominant right or left hand. He will use this hand to hold a pencil or a crayon with a "pincer" grip (the traditional grip used to hold a pen or pencil), and write in a fairly legible manner. He is able to write for a purpose and as he gets older, use the space available to write what is required. In addition to writing, during the primary school years, the child may learn to play sports, a musical instrument, or develop an interest in specific craft activities that require refined tool use and hand skill. For a child with delayed fine motor or eye–hand coordination skills, this can become an area of great frustration.

Naturally, a child will not willingly participate in activities that cause frustration or even discomfort. This may be the beginning of a slippery slope. As the child resists using his hands, the natural practice that could enhance these skills is avoided. Therefore, the child's hand skills are underdeveloped and his functional skills become increasingly worse. Take heart! It is important to remember that although children with ASDs may not follow the timeline other children do, they will most likely reach the same end result—to be able to accomplish tasks independently.

Visual tracking is following something by moving the eyes only. The head or body does not need to move when visually following a person or an object. Visual tracking is especially difficult for children with ASDs, as they often have an aversion to looking at others, but they will look at their favorite item! Hold that item and see if the child will reach for it or just look at it as you move it up/down and side to side. If the child understands, ask him to look only with his eyes and not turn his head. Other activities that will encourage eye–hand coordination include shape matching, and following a rolling ball or a favorite car or truck along a path.

Some things move naturally. Examples of these moving objects are light-weight mobiles that swing in the softest breeze. When the child follows an object with his eye, whether it is something blowing in the breeze or a toy, he is exercising his visual system. If the child has a favorite car or train, move that toy. While playing on the floor with the child, drive that train in a wide circle or even a figure of eight pattern. As the child watches you play, he is exercising his eye muscles. Rolling a ball back and forth as you sit on the floor facing the child is great fun. It is a satisfying feeling to have the ball come straight to the child, and then watch as you collect the rolled ball. To create a successful experience, sit very close to the child and roll the ball in both directions until he understands the idea.

The figure of eight is a favorite shape for occupational therapists. It allows the child to cross the mid-line or the center of the body, and causes both sides of the brain to communicate. Playing with cars and trucks and moving them in a figure of eight pattern (as in a toy race track) is an excellent way to develop eye–hand coordination skill. However, limit the time the child spends participating in the lining up of items as this reinforces the use of toys as mere generic pieces or objects and does not encourage the understanding of the purpose of toys in the environment.

A word of caution: It is important for all of us, especially those with ASDs, to have "down time." So after a few minutes of following his favorite truck moving around in a figure of eight pattern, allow the child to line it up with his other trucks.

Videogames are not the answer to eye–hand coordination challenges. While many children become experts at various games, and develop impressive skill at maneuvering buttons to make video images move, these skills cannot be transferred to other functional areas of life. When a child develops greater strength when viewing items from the distance from the couch to the television screen, this strength will not generalize to other distances. He needs to develop visual skills at closer and further distances, such as when constructing a puzzle or playing catch. Videogames do not help the child put the top back on the tube of toothpaste and turn it so that it is closed.

In addition, extended periods of time in a sedentary position do not allow for strengthening of the core muscles. Core muscles are the muscles in the centre of the body. These muscles are important for posture, breathing and overall good health. When a child does not have strong core muscles he may experience back aches, overall fatigue, poor gross and fine motor skills, and a diminished sense of wellbeing.

Playing catch with a friend is one of the best ways for the child to develop eye–hand coordination. Hitting a balloon in the air or back and forth with another person is great fun. This can be done at any age, and the give-and-take nature of the activity encourages socialization. Other sports that also encourage the development of this skill are tennis, softball, or ping pong, to name a few.

Bilateral coordination

Bilateral coordination refers to using both sides of the body together in a manner that allows someone to accomplish a functional task. This skill develops without our attention, and we use it naturally in just about every functional task. It begins to develop in infants. Walking, tying shoes, running, skipping, walking up and down the stairs, cutting paper with scissors, stringing beads, and touch typing are examples of activities that require bilateral coordination. Riding a tricycle is great exercise and allows the lower body to move in a coordinated way, while the upper body holds on and develops a strong upright posture and strength.

Infants

As the baby begins to develop bilateral coordination, the typically developing infant will hold an object in one hand and manipulate it with the other. For example, he may crawl into the kitchen cabinet, and hold a pot while banging it with a spoon with the other hand; he may also take apart pop beads or blocks. Learning to walk is a great example of bilateral coordination—one foot then the other moves forward as the child naturally works against gravity to gain his upright posture.

Singing songs with movement games such as "Row, Row, Row Your Boat" as you hold each of the child's hands and have him face you encourages growth in this area. As you sing this song, move his hands (or feet) in a reciprocal manner, pulling one, while pushing the other. This exercises each side of the body, and alerts it to moving in a coordinated way.

Toddlers

During this time, toddlers begin to develop a dominant hand. With this development, the typical child may be seen putting together simple toys with three or four parts. As he develops, the child will start to use both hands in a coordinated way to unbutton his clothing, use scissors while holding paper, or spread cream cheese on a bagel. A fun activity to encourage the use of both hands together and increase body awareness at the same time is to have the child trace his own hand (see 'Let's make a paper me' on pp.28–29).

There are other ways to encourage bilateral coordination in toddlers. One example is allowing the child to help with tasks around the house. If a ball of string or an unplugged extension cord needs to be wound up, having the child do this will strengthen his bilateral coordination. Tying knots in ribbon when it is time to wrap a package is also a good coordination task. Learning to tie a bow is even better. Simply tearing paper, if you have something that needs to be shredded, is great fun for young children. The opposite directions the hands move when tearing a piece of paper support bilateral coordination. This task gets the child involved in a family activity and helps him gain skill. He may really enjoy the sound of the paper tearing and the mess he creates. If you want to get creative, children can make mosaic pictures out of paper pieces they have torn.

Children

The typical child is able to use small scissors effectively. He is able to dress and undress and use common clothing fasteners, cut food, and use tools (such as a screwdriver), and write legibly.

For children who need help in this area, there are many ways to incorporate bilateral coordination into daily life. To increase bilateral coordination, encourage the child to participate in activities that require the smooth use of both sides of the body, such as skipping, jumping jacks, making beaded necklaces, playing "cat's cradle," or playing with a "slinky."

Offer opportunities for the child to cross the mid-line of his body. Tracing or drawing a figure of eight design or any other design with intersecting lines is an excellent exercise. Start big and move to small spaces. Place two pillows on the floor and walk around them in a figure of eight pattern.

Start in the center and move up and to the left. Place your hands on the child's hips or shoulders and move him along this way, or have him hold on to the adult as he moves along with the adult in front. Then progress to drawing the shape that was just walked. Make sure that the child does not draw each half of the design separately, but in one continuous line. Using his index finger to create a figure of eight pattern design in rice or sand, or creating one out of clay, is also appropriate. This multi-sensory approach is very effective for learning.

The child is seeing the shape, feeling the movement, and experiencing the touch of different textures. Drawing an X shape is also a great way to get both sides of the brain active. It is really fun to do this in the bath tub with shaving cream on the wall!

Provide opportunities for gross motor planning through participation in activities such as ring toss, games of catch with varying size balls, and obstacle course maneuvers that involve both upper and lower extremities. Skipping, however, is a very difficult bilateral coordination task. Encourage the child to hop first on one foot and then the other.

For school-age children, not being embarrassed can be all consuming. Children with ASDs have stood out as being different for most of their lives, and nothing will make them stand out more than being "uncoordinated." Many children avoid activities that require bilateral coordination so their poor skills in this area are not evident.

Of course, as with any activity, the less it is practiced the less skill is developed. So, the question becomes, "How do we engage the growing young person in pursuits that will hone these skills?" Here, as much as in any other skill area, a feeling of success is important, as is providing fun activities that encourage work in this area. The challenge is to create success experiences and build on those. Start small. Can the child toss a ball in the air and catch it? If a ball is too fast, start with a bean bag. Once the bean bag is no problem, increase the challenge by getting the child to clap once after the toss up, before the bag is caught. Once this is mastered, the child should clap more than once.

When the child is able to clap three times consistently (three attempts in a row), it is time to advance to the ball. Continue this process with the ball. Once the self-catching with three claps is mastered, it is time to play catch with a friend. This simple reciprocal activity not only enhances the coordination skills of the child, but goes a long way to developing social skills. Bilateral coordination can also be developed by any activity that uses both sides of the body in a coordinated way. Other examples include most craft activities such as stringing beads for a necklace, making pizza dough or tortillas, and more whole body exercises such as jumping jacks. It is never too late to increase a skill level. Riding a bicycle, even a stationary one, is a great idea at any age.

Coordination is an innate skill that develops with natural play activity. It occurs when the body responds to positional, movement, or visual challenges. As the child responds to those challenges, his nervous system, muscles, and bones become more coordinated. When the challenging play activity does not occur naturally, because the child has an ASD, the carer can step in and provide the opportunities and information for the stimulation that the nervous system requires to develop.

This information is provided through the encouragement of play activities in which the child will actively engage. Providing encouragement and opportunities through fun activities that the child actively participates in is the key to developing coordination and an overall sense of wellbeing in the child. Through the activities presented, the carer understands the purpose of each play activity and knows the sort of response to expect as the child gains skills.

Chapter 3

Fine Motor Skills

The ideas presented in this chapter are provided in a chronological order and sequence. Please note that not all children proceed through development in the same order. Use these ideas as guidelines to demonstrate the hand skills the child will eventually achieve. Children with ASDs do achieve these skills. The child may be able to use these hand skills at a later age than other children, but he will be able. The goal throughout this book is to provide some ideas that encourage functional skill development, while providing some fun activities and interactions. Understanding that the child has certain preferences is important. Various options are presented so that you and the child may discover his likes and dislikes.

A word of caution: Even when a child expresses a preference, keep offering him a variety. One day he may surprise you and choose differently. At times it may appear that the skills the child once had are now gone. They are not gone. Those skills are just not currently being expressed. The child will once again use the skills he seems to have lost, when the time is right. He will once again be able to hold a toothbrush, button his shirt, or connect the building blocks.

"Fine motor skills" is a term used to describe how hands work. Many therapists and medical professionals use this term to talk about the muscles, coordination, and dexterity of the hands. The hands are observed when they are doing something, not when they are at rest. Most of the activities we *do* on a daily basis can be categorized as fine motor skills. Some of these skills include dressing, hygiene, school, and craft activities. As the child develops he uses his hands to learn about the world and about himself. Children with ASDs may be reluctant to use their hands for a variety of reasons. Some of those reasons include lack of interest, weakness, or a dislike of how things feel. The delay of hand use causes the many small muscles of the hand to remain immature or weak. Encouraging hand use in a variety of ways allows the child to explore the world. As he is exploring the world, he is learning and helping those hand and finger muscles to grow strong.

When left alone, without encouragement, the baby who will later be diagnosed as having an ASD may not play with his own hands, which is the first thing infants do to develop hand skills. The typical baby discovers his hands when one day, as he is moving his hands for no apparent reason, one hand touches the other. Then he begins to grasp and hold his own hands.

This grasping motion and finger play develop the small muscles of the hand. Another benefit of this finger play is that the baby begins to learn that he has five fingers on each hand and that each finger moves separately. He may have already discovered his thumb! Soon he will bring his hands into his mouth where further discovery and exploration takes place.

Often babies and young children will bring their hands close to their faces and then further away. This is a way for them to experiment with their vision. The typically developing infant may lose interest in sucking his thumb by six months. Children with ASDs may not develop an interest in sucking until they reach preschool age. Those children may be observed sucking on their shirt collar and other non-food items. Children with ASDs may not participate in early finger play or sucking discovery so before they reach preschool or age three their hand skills may already be delayed.

Many children's songs have hand and finger movements that help with fine motor development. These movements work to increase strength, dexterity, and refine finger movements. When singing these songs, move the child's hands so his fingers are moving along with the music. Choose a variety of songs. Some tunes use the entire hand while others focus on individual fingers. You will learn a great deal about how the child uses his hands when you ask him simply to give you the "thumbs up" sign. Ask the child to point at his nose. Is he using his whole hand to point, or can he isolate his index finger and fold the other fingers into his palm?

Sometimes children are not aware that they have five fingers on each hand. Singing songs and using movements that encourage the touching of the tips of each of the four other fingers with the thumb provides excellent exercise. This is called "opposition." That is, the thumb is touching each tip of an opposing finger. Making the "Okay" sign is using finger opposition with the thumb and index finger. Increasing the child's awareness of his ten fingers and encouraging him to use them individually is the first step in helping him use his hands for other activities. Some of those include writing and buttoning a shirt.

The age-old classic song about the tiny spider, "Incy Wincy Spider," works well for this purpose. The child needs to touch his pinky with the thumb on the opposite hand. This gets all the fingers involved. In addition to finger movements, the child's wrists get exercise with the twisting motions needed to successfully have the spider climb up the waterspout.

The ability to hold on to something and to use it effectively comes after a great deal of learning and development, such as holding a pencil, a crayon, or eating utensil. The hand needs to develop and then learn the proper way to manipulate a tool and use it as intended. This is the essence of a fine motor skill. The hand, of course, is the first tool used. This is no different for children with ASDs than any other child.

At first an infant will grasp a finger or a toy it feels against the palm. This is a natural reflex. Infants do not need to think about this grasp. When a baby is nursing, he will hold the mother's finger that is provided. This allows him to feel calm and begins the process of fine motor development. Children with ASDs may need encouragement to develop their hand skills. Hand and visual skills are interwoven in development. The more the baby or child visually pays attention to an object, the more he will attempt to use his hands to grasp the object and play with it.

Getting the visual attention of the child with an ASD so they want to touch an object is a challenge. Use the concept of "high contrast." High contrast means choosing toys that have a very dark or a very light color. A good combination of colors is black, white, and red. Using toys that have this color combination is more likely to attract the attention of children with ASDs than toys that have more subtle colors. If a baby is at risk of developing an ASD, he may not be interested in the toys presented to him. As the child is reluctant to explore the world with his hands it is easy to see how delays in fine motor skills start very young. For this reason, it is important to encourage the infant to use his hands. The suggestions below provide ideas for increasing hand use in the very young child.

At first the baby will swat at an object that is suspended above him but within his reach. The baby will use his entire arm and his whole body may move in tandem with his arm movement. The baby will most likely use both his arms at once. The baby will eventually grasp the object, at first just as a reflex, and later intentionally. As the baby gains some skill in holding an object, he will bring it to a central view so he can see it. He may even put it in his mouth. He also sees that if the object moves, it may make a sound. If the baby enjoys this sound he will move or shake the toy repeatedly to experience the sound he enjoys. Some children with ASDs are extremely sensitive to sound. They may prefer the sound of one rattle toy over another. It is important to pay attention to this. If you notice that one sound results in a smile or visual attention while the other results in crying or another negative response, respect that tendency. The necessary learning will take place if a pleasing sound is used. If no sound is enjoyed, then eliminate the rattles from the toy box until the baby or child is able to feel more comfortable with a variety of sounds.

The next step the baby takes will be purposefully putting the object into his mouth. As the baby begins to enjoy this activity, he seeks it out. A series of movements that was once an accidental episode of touching and grasping becomes purposeful. Paying attention to when the baby begins to look for the object that he can hold and feel with his mouth provides an important opportunity to encourage learning.

The more success a baby or child demonstrates by overcoming a challenge, the more he is willing to expend the effort to accomplish more and more. This remains true across all ages in the lifespan and all activities. Providing objects that the child can reach for is important. To encourage learning, do not place the object too close or in the child's hand. Rather, place the desired object just far enough away so that he needs to exert a bit of effort to grasp it. When he has done this successfully, he will begin to develop a sense of accomplishment. Success is a great motivator.

If the child does not naturally bring the object or toy to the central view (mid-line) then do it for him. For a baby's eyes to begin to work in a coordinated way, he needs to look at objects in the front and middle of his view. Hold the toy of interest above his nose about six inches (15 cm) from his face and attempt to gain his attention by moving the toy so that sound or light reflections attract his attention. Perhaps the toy has a face and eyes. Remember that toys with high contrast colors are more interesting. Slowly move the object up and down and side to side so the baby follows it with his eyes. Do this for only a few minutes at a time. Try to keep your words or sounds of encouragement to a minimum so as not to overwhelm the baby or child with too much information at once.

The first grip to develop is called a "gross grasp." The entire hand is used. At first the child will use a gross or whole hand grasp to eat a cookie or draw with a crayon. The next step after the whole hand grasp is a more refined grip. This is the grip that is commonly referred to as a "pincer grip." It is used to hold the tab of a zipper, pick up a pea, or hold a pencil. Once the child is able to sit up by himself, his hand development can really advance. Grasping and releasing is the first and most basic skill that develops. Holding objects of various sizes and shapes assures this development and provides a solid foundation for the more refined skills to come.

Often children with ASDs have delayed manipulation skills. Manipulation skills are important for writing, eating, using clothing fasteners, and participating in many leisure activities.

The following provides some fine motor activities designed to help children with ASDs develop fine motor dexterity for tool use. A few things are important to remember, as with all suggested activities. If the proposed activity causes stress, stop it. Do not have the child engage in any activity to the point of fatigue. Allow the child some success experiences and continue with the play as long as it is challenging and holds interest. It is better to stop while the child is demonstrating a good technique than allow him to work to the point where his performance begins to decline.

Foundation skills

Among other things, preschool programs include many hand or fine motor activities. A typical preschool program provides the opportunity for children to engage in various songs with finger movements, building blocks or interlocking blocks, bead stringing, and the use of various textures such as clay, sand, water, or shaving cream. The child is introduced to various writing and expressive tools, such as finger paint, brushes, pencils, crayons, and markers. He is encouraged to use tools such as scissors, hole punches, and tongs, along with eating and cooking utensils.

A preschooler may even have the opportunity to learn to take care of pets, such as feeding fish with a pinch of food or using hammer and nails to build a bird house. At times they may explore sounds made by touching various musical instruments in certain ways with specific finger movements, or holding a guitar pick or drum sticks. Children with ASDs may not explore these opportunities. They may not understand the verbal directions provided. They may also be uncomfortable with being close to their classmates, or too much information may be coming to them at once.

Children with ASDs may have difficulty deciding what information to pay attention to at any one time. They may be working on just feeling comfortable in the room when the teacher and all the other students are done with circle time and the morning "Hello" song and are on to finger painting or weeding the classroom garden.

The selection of activities below provides a structured way to present these hand skill activities to the preschool child with an ASD. They include the hand movements involved, the supplies needed, and the way to present the instructions. In general if the activity is a craft project then an example of a finished project is nice to have, but certainly not necessary. Children with ASDs do well, in general, when they can copy a movement or activity. So have fun, get messy, and remember, "It's the process not the product!"

It is important to try to understand the point of view of the child with an ASD. Although you may enjoy displaying a finished product, the display may have a different meaning for children with ASDs. For the child, the experience of creating may be of interest and the final masterpiece of no interest at all. When working with a child with ASD, be aware of the environment. When we discuss community skills, we will go into detail about the environment. For now, working on hand skills is sufficient. The television or radio should not be on and multi-tasking should be avoided if at all possible. Spend 10 to 20 minutes focusing on the skill and pay attention to the child and what he is doing at that moment.

The pinch

Have you noticed how many times a day you move your thumb and index finger together? You do this when you pick up a pen, when you button a shirt, or when you pluck a tissue from a box. This is one of the most universal and important hand movements.

The pinch advances from using all five fingers to using two. In general, you can help the child to develop this skill by providing him with objects to pick up in a series from larger to smaller. The larger items may be as large as a table-top tennis ball (ping pong ball), or a one-inch (2.5 cm) block, and the small objects may be as tiny as a pea or even smaller. If you are providing tiny things to pick up, and the child has a tendency to put things into his mouth, make sure that the small items are edible, or at the very least, not toxic.

Activities that have a bit of resistance work well to develop the small muscles of the hand. These muscles are important in the development of finger dexterity. A good activity to develop hand and pinch muscle strength is making pictures with rubber bands. On a grid of nails, stretch the bands over the nails to create a picture. The finished result is not important. The accomplishment of stretching the bands from one nail to the other is very satisfying. The child may be making a picture that is beautiful to him and not conform to any idea of art that you are familiar with. Allow the child his free expression while working with his hands. A weaving loom is also a good choice for using hand muscles in combination with the pinch. Here are some other ideas that are fun and can be done with common materials.

THE FUZZY PICTURE

Supplies needed for this activity include the following:

- colored construction paper
- wax paper
- white school glue
- tempera paint (two or three colors)
- cotton balls (or a large piece of cotton)—natural fibers are preferable to synthetics such as polyester for comfort.

1.   Choose a colored sheet of 8.5 x 11 inches (Letter or A4 size) construction paper for the background of the picture.

2.   Squeeze a small pool of different color paint on the wax paper.

3.   Pick up one cotton ball from the bag, and hold it between the thumb and index finger of each hand. Pull the cotton ball apart. If the child is at the stage of using more fingers than only the thumb and index finger for his pinch, this is alright. As he gains skill, a more refined pinch will develop.

4.   When the cotton ball is stretched or pulled apart as desired, dip it in the white glue and place it on a contrasting colored piece of construction paper. Continue to make a design with the various shapes of cotton balls.

5.   When the design is complete, take another cotton ball, and hold it between the thumb and index finger. Dip the cotton ball into the small pool of desired color on wax paper and "paint" the cotton ball that has been glued in place. This painting can be achieved by actual brushing with the cotton ball or simple dabbing. The cotton ball with paint may also be used as a paintbrush to add color to the paper directly. Use a different cotton ball for each color; some of the fuzzy shapes may be left white.

6.   Wait for these creations to dry and hang them up for all to see. This is an excellent activity for children with ASDs and fun for any child. This teaches the children a sequence, the experience of various textures, and provides an opportunity for them to create something that may proudly be displayed.

The use of high contrast colors will keep children with ASDs interested longer. Avoid light and subtle contrast colors such as pastels or shades of one primary color (primary colors are red, blue, and yellow).

LET'S MAKE DINNER

Even very young children can participate in preparing food for the family or for their own snack. Here is one idea that everyone will enjoy.

Ingredients you will need:

- pizza dough (this is easy to find already prepared at the market)
- non-stick cookie sheet
- dry seasonings: salt, garlic powder, oregano, pepper, sugar, and cinnamon—in small bowls. Use the flavors that the child especially enjoys.

Instructions:

1. Pinch a small amount of the dough between your thumb and index finger.
2. Dip the dough into the seasoning of choice.
3. Drop the balls onto the cookie sheet, about one inch (2.5 cm) apart.
4. Bake according to directions on the dough package.

The child will be very happy that he was able to participate in preparing part of dinner or a snack. The shapes created will be uneven and that is fine. If the child expresses a need to have the dough shapes even and round, then feel free to have him roll the dough he has pinched into a ball. Other pinch ideas in the kitchen include shelling peas, tearing lettuce, or peeling citrus fruit.

MACARONI OR BEAN FACE

Children of all ages enjoy making pictures using dry food ingredients. The supplies for this are simple: paper, white glue, and beans or pasta. Just make sure that the paper and the beans or pasta are different colors. The goal here is to make sure that the colors contrast. Have the child pick up one small bean at a time, and glue it in place.

Children with ASDs will be successful if they have an outline to follow. With direction from the child, draw shapes or a face. Even a straight or curved line works well for this craft. If the child is working on drawing straight lines or crossed lines, using the same lines will help to reinforce that learning. Have the child glue the beans along the lines you have drawn for this activity. This provides the child with a comfortable structured activity. As he works with gluing along his pattern, he is able to see how far he has progressed and how far he has to go. If you think that a whole face or large or complex shape will be overwhelming, simply start with a circle. You can even work on this in stages. For example, if you are creating a face or a whole person, just work on one part at a time, and come back to the project another day.

It is important that the child stays engaged and interested in the project. When you notice that he is losing interest, let the child know that you are aware of this, and begin your cleanup routine. Having the child participate in a cleanup routine, even if he is not able to do a thorough job, is important. As the child becomes accustomed to cleaning up after all activities he is learning an important life skill.

AROUND THE HOUSE AND GARDEN

All plants at one time or another require pinching off of dead leaves or blossoms. No matter the environment you live in, there are always weeds to be pulled! Having the child help with this chore teaches him a great skill and allows him to participate in a needed task. Show the child which plant parts need to be pinched off. Use simple explanations such as, "the brown ones" or "the dry ones." As always, demonstrate what you want done first and then allow the child to copy you. It is a good idea to keep him away from your prize roses, just in case a mistake is made.

TOOL USE

Small tongs or chopsticks can be fastened together to form child-size tongs. These may be used as a fun way to eat small bits of food. The squeezing motion of the tongs strengthens the small muscles of the hand. These muscles are important for small refined tasks.

Wrist position

Paying attention to the child's wrist position when using his hands is important. A strong wrist position will prevent fatigue as the child gets older and learns to write. The proper writing position is with the pinky side of the hand down on the paper and the wrist bent slightly back. The writing tool is to be held comfortably in the thumb web space at approximately a 45-degree angle to the paper. The thumb and index finger "pinch" the pencil. When writing with a pencil on paper, only small finger movements are needed to create letters and numbers. The weaker the hand, the more movement will be seen in the entire arm. A very weak child may even use his shoulder and hold his elbow up at an awkward angle when writing, or write with his wrist bent forward.

EASEL

Having an easel set up for the child to write, draw, paint, or make spongy paintings encourages the slight bend backwards that is important to encourage the strength and proper hand position needed later on when he begins to write. The child will be standing when he uses the easel. If an easel is not available, paper may be fastened to the wall to provide the child with an upright position for writing or drawing. Make sure the paper is directly in front of the child at shoulder height so that he can write or with his arm bent only slightly. Reaching too high may be uncomfortable and create very tired arms while not teaching proper wrist positioning for writing.

LARGE BINDER AND SEATED ACTIVITIES

Secure writing or drawing paper to the thick closed side of a three ring binder with a large diameter. Depending on the age and size of the child, use a binder that is one to three inches (2.5 to 7.5 cm) wide. Place the binder on the table with the opening towards the child (the binder is on the table so that it opens top to bottom, rather than side to side). Secure paper to the outside of the binder with tape. This provides a slanted surface that encourages the proper wrist position for writing. Allow the child to experiment with different writing positions. He may write or draw. Copy the marks he makes as a way to show him that he is communicating with you. Notice if his wrist position looks comfortable. The wrist should be tipped with a slight backwards bend. You may notice that the child is very comfortable in this position and more willing to write this way. If this is the case, commercially available slant boards are available specifically for this use.

Make it noticeable

High visual contrast is important for children with ASDs. It may be said that they need a lot of information to get their attention. If you are using white paper, then use black or dark primary colors for writing or drawing. If the child prefers to write or draw on colored paper, make sure that he has distinctive and contrasting colors for his creations.

Right or left handed?

By the age of three it is easy to tell if a child is right or left handed. He will be reaching for his favorite food items or toys with the preferred hand. Often he will reach across the center of his body with his preferred hand to pick up what he wants. This reaching across the body is called "crossing the mid-line."

If the child is not reaching across his body, but reaches for things on the right side with his right hand, and the left side with his left hand, this does not mean he is ambidextrous. More than likely, he has not yet fully established a right or left hand dominance. Establishing a dominant hand is an important milestone. Having a dominant hand supports learning to read and write and overall coordination. The establishment of a dominant hand is a sign of growth and development.

If you notice that the child is not reaching across the center of his body for items or to point at things, you can help with his development. Reaching across the center of the body is important because it helps the left and right sides of the brain communicate with each other. This helps the child know what his whole body is doing and for him to feel more balanced.

The time to encourage the child to establish a dominant hand is when he is showing some signs of having a preference, but is somewhat resistant to using the preferred hand consistently. If you think the child is right or left handed and sometimes uses the other hand to reach for objects so that he does not have to expend the extra effort to reach across the center of his body, try these activities. The more the child reaches across the center of his body while doing everyday activities, the more his brain is developing. This is by no means a return to the time when left-handed children were forced to use their right hands. It is just a way to help the child along the way to maturity whether he is right or left handed. Here are some ideas you and the child may enjoy.

FAVORITE FOOD FEST

Whether it is chicken nuggets, cheerios, or grapes, most children have a favorite finger food. Have the child sit at the table facing forward. Place a plate directly in front of him with his favorite finger food in a line or a circle around the plate. The child will naturally reach for the food and begin to eat. Gently hold the "non-dominant" hand as you casually and quietly talk with the child, and encourage him to enjoy his snack. Or you can remain silent and just enjoy each other's company.

If you do not feel right about holding his hand, you can give him a favorite little truck or car to hold on to with the non-dominant hand. You will observe the child reaching to the opposite side of the plate for the food item he desires. Notice if the child is turning his body as he reaches. If he is turning his body, this means he is resistant to crossing the mid-line. Simply reposition him so that he is sitting in a straight direction. Use the positioning corrections and non-dominant hand distractions for no more than five minutes the first day. Keep at it a few times a day as a natural part of snack or mealtimes. This skill will develop over time with a little help and encouragement.

PUZZLE TIME

Jigsaw puzzles are a family favorite, and they help develop many skills. This activity is helpful whether the puzzle contains five or 500 pieces. Puzzles are a great way to develop visual and position capacities and encourage hand dominance. They are also a great way to foster socialization and develop a concrete and lasting model of hard work. To encourage crossing the mid-line while working on a puzzle, determine a top and bottom and the right and left sides of the picture. As the child works on the puzzle, encourage him to stay in one place. He may choose to work on one side of the puzzle or the other. He may even enjoy working on the puzzle with the picture upside down.

The important point is that once he has decided his position for the current puzzle session, he will stay in that spot. The child may not walk around the table to fit his found piece. Reaching across or to the other side encourages crossing the mid-line. Again, as with any exercise, start slowly and build up. Encourage the child to stay in his "spot" for one or two minutes at first. After this time is over, if the child wishes, he may move around the table to fit the puzzle pieces in place.

The last thing we want is for the child to become frustrated with such a fun pastime. Frustration will turn a joyful activity into one to be avoided. Know the child's signs of frustration, and stop the challenge before he becomes resistant to puzzle building. If the child becomes frustrated with not being allowed to move from his "spot," allow a few puzzle sessions to happen without attention to crossing the mid-line. Then, try again.

READING TIME

Reading is one of the favorite activities of parents and children of all ages. It provides a great opportunity every day to encourage crossing the mid-line with fingers and eyes. Here is a simple activity to do every time you read with the child. Hold the index finger of his dominant hand. Hold the child's finger for as long as he will allow. Move his finger from left to right as you read along. Hold his finger while you point to parts of the picture in all areas of the page. Make sure you point out parts that are on all sides and top and bottom. As the child understands directions, ask him to point to items that are in all areas.

When the child actively participates, great learning will take place. After you have moved the child's finger, observing different words or parts of the picture, give him a turn. See if the child will move his finger across the page, independently. Learning and development that sticks with the child happens when he is active in the experience more than if he is passive.

BATH TIME

Time in the bath tub provides a great opportunity for learning and developing skills. Apply a few handfuls of shaving cream to the wall. Spread it within reach of the child. Make a rectangular shape with the cream so that when a finger is moved through it, the shape is obvious.

Allow the child just to play so he can see and feel how he can make marks with one finger drawn through the shaving cream. After the child has touched the cream, and understands how to make marks, the teaching can begin. Simply draw a large "X." Encourage the child to copy this shape. After he is able to copy the "X" demonstrate a figure of eight shape. This is simply the number eight on its side.

FIGURE OF EIGHT: RACE TRACK TO ORGANIZATION

The classic race car track is a figure of eight. The race car moves across an "X" in the middle of the track, going up and down along oblong ellipse shapes on either side. Usually the child uses a race track on the floor. He follows the car and if he can be encouraged to use one hand, perhaps by holding another car in the other hand, he is getting great exercise and crossing the mid-line.

The more his eyes and hands work together to cross the mid-line of his visual field and his body, the more organized his brain will become. This simply means that information from the environment will be more efficiently understood. If a race track is not available, any path that creates the shape of the eight will work.

WALKING IN A FIGURE OF EIGHT

The figure of eight shape is wonderful in a very small space, either with the fingertips in the bath or with the whole body. This walk may be done indoors or out. When indoors, all you will need are two objects such as small pillows or stuffed toys.

Place the objects on the floor about three feet (a meter) apart. Beginning in the center between the two objects, walk up and to the left, then around the top of the pillow on the left. Continue walking around the pillow until you get to the center. Once you reach the center, cross over and begin to walk around the top of the pillow on the right side. Continue walking around the pillows, making sure that you cross in the center, avoiding making two circles next to each other. If the child will not follow you, perhaps you can steer him gently with your hands on his hips. If steering is not an option, carrying the child works as well.

If the child is carried as you walk around in the figure of eight formation, he will get the sensation of crossing the mid-line, and his eyes will have the opportunity to practice visual tracking in this way. When the child is able to follow an adult who is walking in the figure of eight formation, there are many ways to make this exercise more interesting. Have the child march as he walks around, and declare "left!", "right!" as he goes along. This reinforces the identity of either side of the body. To provide even more information, have the child tap each knee as it rises during marching.

Slow and rhythmic movements allow the child's brain to pay attention to the new information. Slow and controlled movements are much more of a challenge than quick movements that do not need thought as they are performed. It is better to do an activity correctly for a shorter period of time than incorrectly for more time.

When playing outside, walking in a figure of eight pattern can be done between two trees or large rocks.

Progressing hand skills and tool use

Gone are the days when kindergarten was all about free play, when time was spent in imaginary play in the "house" and in the block area, with some time set aside for finger painting and snacks. These days children are expected to enter kindergarten with some "school skills." These fine motor skills include writing their names, the letters of the alphabet, and numbers. By the end of kindergarten, children are expected to write simple sentences, on a line, with all the letters approximately the same size. This presents a special set of challenges for children with ASDs. They may not have developed the fine motor skills to hold the pencil correctly or to be able to pay attention to the lines on the writing paper.

Most if not all instruction in a typical classroom is provided verbally. The teacher tells the children what to do, and they are expected to "follow directions." For many children on the Autism Spectrum the use of verbal directions is a challenge. Children with ASDs may do much better when following a set of visual directions.

This means that the teacher will need to demonstrate each step of a project before expecting the child to follow suit. Teachers may also have a set of diagrams or pictures of the project for each activity of the day. These simple accommodations may make the difference between success and failure in the classroom for children with ASDs.

Fine motor expectations become increasingly more difficult as the child increases his participation in school. Activities often include multiple steps and tool use. Below are more interesting and engaging activities that will provide "school-like" experiences so that when these are presented in class, the child will have some familiarity with these activities as well as a level of skill.

Scissors

Using scissors is a very important task as the child becomes more involved in school. Using a "thumbs up" position is the first step to proper scissor use. The basic concept of opening and closing the scissors needs to be understood before successful paper cutting occurs.

There are many types of adaptive scissors. Some provide an automatic opening sequence, so that the child simply squeezes the scissors closed to make the cut, and progresses along the line. Some other scissor adaptations have an extra set of holes, so that an assisting adult may do the actual work of opening and closing the scissors, while the child's hand simply goes along for the ride.

One important element of scissor use is the idea of a dominant hand and a non-dominant (helper) hand. The hand not using the scissors is an important helper for this skill. The child should be encouraged to hold the card or paper he is snipping with his "helper" hand to keep it steady. As the child gains skill with his scissor skills, the "helper" hand turns the paper so that the hand cutting with the scissors can maintain the forward and thumbs up position. The sequence of cutting skill development is as follows:

1. Snip the edges of a stiff paper or card.

2. Starting on the edge of a card, snip along a thick straight line that needs two or three snips.

3. Starting on the edge of a card, snip along a curved line, then a line with two or three curves, and a line with edges like sharks' teeth.

4. Cut out a triangle, square, and a circle.

For a child with ASD, make sure that the lines to be cut out are a dark contrast to the paper he is cutting.

Cutting a variety of different papers such as thick file folders or thin binder paper also increases skill.

CUT AND PASTE

Cutting and pasting activities demonstrate an understanding of the material being presented. Many times the pieces being cut out are from the same paper upon which the cut pieces are to be placed. For the child with ASD, this may not provide enough contrast for him to see the difference between the piece he has cut out and the target spot for the pasting.

A useful accommodation is to provide papers of contrasting colors. With a dark color, outlining the shapes or words to be cut out also provides sufficient contrast. These accommodations provide the child with a higher chance of success as he completes the required activity. A fun activity to do at home or at school is to make a collage. This will give children with ASDs a chance to learn and develop an important skill while enjoying their special interest. Here are some guidelines to follow:

1. Lay out a piece of dark paper for the background of the collage.

2. Provide a few magazines that have pictures of the child's special interest (e.g. cars or trains).

3. Have the child point to a desired picture to be cut out.

4. Draw a thick black shape around the picture (the shape will be determined by the shape of the picture).

5. If the child has the skill, encourage him to circle or draw any shape around the pictures of interest.

6. Have the child cut out the pictures circled.

7. Allow the child to organize the cut pictures however he likes onto the dark paper.

8. Once the pictures are laid out, have the child apply glue from a glue stick onto the cut pictures and place them one at a time onto the background piece.

9. When the child decides the picture is finished, display his work for all to see.

Coloring in shapes and spaces

"Stay inside the lines" is repeated many times a day in classrooms around the world. Although we are not striving to create or reinforce perfectionism, it is important to "color inside the lines" sometimes. When a child colors within a specific space, he is demonstrating an understanding of where specific spaces or shapes begin and end. When he can successfully fill in a space, he is also demonstrating that he is seeing the lines and his hands are cooperating with the instructions from his brain. To help children with ASDs see the spaces clearly, the following activity is recommended:

1. Outline a shape with a dark and contrasting colored line.

2. Make a raised border in which to color with wax sticks or yarn that you have glued down with white glue and prepared for this purpose. You can also use large plastic stencils for this purpose.

3. Tracing shapes is a good way for the child to understand the idea of specific shapes. Tracing the child's hand as he places it flat on a piece of paper is a great way for him to see the shapes of objects in the environment and increase his awareness of his body parts. It is also fun to trace other objects. Try tracing around a favorite cup, pencil box, or toy. The child will find it fascinating to see the outlined shape of a familiar object.

Writing legibly on the line

Even though we are entering a world where written communication is increasingly done on a keyboard, handwriting continues to be an important skill that the child needs to learn. There are many options for writing tools. As we will discuss in Chapter 4 on senses, the child may have specific preferences. Try many different shapes, sizes, and textures of pencils and crayons until you find the ones the child will use. To write legibly, the child needs to write on a line and letters need to be formed correctly. Those correctly formed letters need to be of uniform size.

The child also needs to apply the appropriate amount of pressure to the writing tool so the letters are visible and the tip of the pencil does not break. Many skills are involved in the writing process. To help the child, you can follow this sequence:

1. Have the child trace and then copy lines, shapes, letters, and numbers.

2. Begin with vertical and horizontal lines. Turn those lines into crossed lines, then a square and a triangle, and finally a circle, an X, and a diamond with diagonal lines.

3. When the child successfully copies the shapes you have demonstrated in a designated area, proceed to letters.

4. Begin with upper case letters as they are mostly straight lines, and then proceed to lower case letters.

5. The first "word" a child learns to write is his first name.

6. To reinforce writing on a line, make sure the lines are a dark contrast or even raised so that the child gets the physical reinforcement of staying on the line when writing and is aware of crossing the line when he moves over a bump.

There are different letter formation style alphabets in use today. It is a good idea to contact the child's school and ask for a sample of the alphabet being used so that you can work on the same letter formation.

Turning the page

Being able to turn the page is an important fine motor skill. This skill involves finger movement and the touch sense that only one page is being turned at a time. Some children with ASDs have a difficult time turning the pages of a book.

The difficulty may be the result of poor finger dexterity, or because the child does not like the way a single page feels on the tips of his fingers. No matter the reason or the discomfort level, turning pages is an important skill. To encourage page turning, have the child turn the pages while you are reading his favorite book. This way, the child is very motivated to see what is on the next page. Although it may feel uncomfortable, he will be distracted and motivated enough to overcome this feeling by the desire to see the next page. Children have an amazing ability to use their minds to overcome many obstacles.

It is important that children with ASDs do as much for themselves in every setting. Increasing your awareness of these little tasks and increasing your expectations of the child's skills helps him become more independent. When a child is very reluctant to turn the page, using a pencil may help. Have him hold the pencil so that the eraser is on the page, and use the grip of the eraser to turn the page.

Following the reading

Following along as the teacher reads aloud is a common activity in class. This provides children with ASDs with the visual information they most likely prefer. Most children with ASDs have difficulty learning when the information is no more than provided through their auditory system. That is, if a teacher only presents information by speaking, the child might not be able to learn; it would be better if he could see the information, as well as hear it. Adding a visual component provides the child with a better chance of learning. Practicing at home and in other settings outside of school is a good way to work on this skill.

When reading at home with the child, have him use his index finger to follow along. This is the same method described earlier (see p.33). If using his index finger is too difficult, the child can take a piece of blank paper and hold it under the line being read. As you come to the end of the line, the child moves the paper down so that the next line is exposed.

The best way to know if the child understands what was being read to him is to ask questions about the material. A child with ASD may not be able to tell you verbally what he has learned. Give the child the option of drawing a picture depicting information that was just learned. Allowing the child to express himself in this manner reinforces his learning and self-esteem. It is important for all of us to know that we are being understood.

A word about hand strength

As the world becomes more technologically advanced, so do our children. Perhaps the child uses a tool that has a touch screen and this has become an effective way for him to communicate, follow a schedule, or complete a task independently. That is terrific, and should be encouraged!

Think about the different amount of hand and finger strength required to use a manual typewriter versus a touch screen keyboard. Even considering that difference, a certain amount of hand strength is important.

There will be times when the child will need to open a food container independently, such as in the lunch room. Or perhaps he may need to use a push pin to display his latest accomplishment on the class cork board. There are many times throughout the day when a certain amount of hand strength is necessary to accomplish a functional task. Allow the child the opportunity to use his hands before you do a task for him. If he is not able to do it—opening the milk container, for example—open it halfway and ask him if he can complete the task. Repeat this strategy with all containers and packages.

This life skill is especially important during lunch away from home. Giving the child the chance to open packages and containers communicates a strong message. He is learning from this experience that he is the one who can provide for his own needs and that he is expected to be capable of doing so. Be patient. This may take years of practice, but with persistence and consistency the child will increase his self-reliance in this important area of life.

Too often the child becomes very good at asking for help and so does not experience the joy of independent accomplishment. We are very good at teaching children with ASDs to say, "Help please." We are so happy that he is communicating his needs that we overlook the bigger picture. We do not always teach him to recognize when he really does need help in contrast to when he needs to put effort into trying the task himself. Consider this a challenge to "sit on your own hands." Allow the child to experience the effort and trials and errors we must all go through before we learn and reach a level of competency.

All the activities that have been highlighted above can work to increase hand strength. The key to increasing strength of any kind is physical resistance and repetition. Here are some more ideas that may be fun to explore with the child.

Nail face picture

With a scrap of wood about one inch thick (2.5 cm), 12 inches (30 cm) wide, and 18 inches (45 cm) long, some two-inch (5 cm) penny nails, and a small hammer, you can make all sorts of designs.

1. Using chalk or permanent markers, draw a happy face or a simple geometric shape on the wood.

2. Show the child how to hold the nail in place while using the hammer to hammer it into the wood about halfway down.

3. If the child is unable to hold the nail while hammering then start each nail and allow him to finish hammering it down. This will strengthen the large muscle of the arm as well as improve eye–hand coordination.

Hole punch activities

1. Using a standard silver one-punch hole punch can greatly increase overall grip strength.

2. Use colored paper, and let the child explore the kinds of designs he can make with the hole punch.

3. Draw geometric designs or letters for him to follow and punch holes in.

4. Fold three or four pieces of paper in half, as if creating a book, and have the child punch holes about ½ inch (1 cm) in from the fold. Thread twine into these two or three holes to "bind" the book.

5. Use the book for other writing or drawing projects.

Let's find the good stuff

For this activity you will need clay, play dough, or commercially available putty that is designed for therapy, and some small items such as small coins, beads, or beans. The more dense and stiff the clay, the harder it will be to use, so to increase strength, start with softer material and increase the density as the child gains strength. Before you begin this activity, roll the clay or putty into a ball shape to warm it up.

1. Use a ball of the putty. The size of the ball should fit easily into the palm of the child's hand.

2. Insert or "hide" five or ten items inside the putty.

3. Allow the child to see you insert the items.

4. Have the child reach into the putty and pull out the hidden items.

5. Count each item as the child finds them in the putty by feeling around and pulling them out. Children with ASDs often feel calm when counting. The fact that this game has a definite beginning and ending is also something that the child with an ASD will appreciate. Line up the found items so he can see what he has found.

There are many wonderful ways that children express themselves with their hands. It is important to remember that all children have their own unique sense of expression. The designs that children with ASDs create are their own expressions. Allow them the joy of that expression while they are building skills. You may even gain a bit of insight into how they view the world.

Chapter 4

Understanding the World through the Senses

There are more senses than the ones we commonly think about. Smell, touch, taste, sight, and sound are important. But there are other senses that are just as important. Other senses include the sense of knowing where you are in space; that is, having a sense without looking of how close or far you are from another person or object. Another sense may be feeling movement and knowing how fast or slow that movement is. Yet another sense is position related; for example, understanding if you are sitting straight up or leaning. The senses that we discuss in this chapter are considered the foundation for experience.

These senses help us understand the world around us and for us to feel comfortable with all the information coming at us. This information is not received solely through the five most common senses but through other senses that provide a lot of other information too. These senses help us understand directions and know where to go, how to move, and what is expected of us.

This chapter provides some ideas for children with ASDs that allows them to clarify the information they are getting from their bodies and the environment. The goal is to guide the child in an understanding of what the world is offering. As he learns, he will be able to interpret his senses and use them to understand the world and feel more comfortable.

Often children on the Autism Spectrum require different sensory experiences to understand the world. They may require more or less than their typical peers. The world is filled with sensory experience. These stimuli are all around us. The hum of the computer, cooking odors, and the vibration from the car as the child rides along are all examples of the many sensory experiences to be had on a typical day. Below are some fun activities you can try to see if they help the child become more relaxed, attentive, and even able to communicate with you more directly. Be aware of any discomfort the child is experiencing. If the child becomes agitated, sweaty, lethargic, or red in the face, neck, or ears, it is time to stop.

Position in space

"Sit up straight," "Look forward," "Write your name on the top left-hand corner of the page." These are all reasonable requests from a teacher. But what if the child does not know what "sit up straight" means or how it feels to sit this way? What if he does not know which direction to turn towards when attempting to "look forward?" What if he does not know where the "top" or the "left" of the paper is located? These are innate understandings that are developed naturally when moving through the world and the senses are developing in a typical manner.

When these senses are delayed or not fully developed the child will have difficulty following directions. Even if he knows the meaning of those directions, he will have trouble demonstrating that understanding with his body or his actions. Learning to understand where one's body is in space is not a paper and pencil task. To learn the sense of where his body is a child must be challenged and so he will respond to maintain his balance or an upright position. Here are some fun ways to help the child learn where his body is in space and how it is moving at home, in the park, or other settings with available equipment.

Swing

Swinging is perhaps the most simple and effective way to teach the child the innate sense of his position. Many children with ASDs do not like to swing and express discomfort at an early age, and so parents avoid swinging. If the child is very reluctant to swing, start slowly, but by all means start.

1. You can hold the child as you, the adult, swings, or even have the child face you with his legs wrapped around you so you can hold him close with one arm.

2. Swing back and forth very slowly, quietly assuring the child that he is safe and you are right there. Holding the child close gives him a lot of security and the more body surface being held, the more secure he will feel.

3. Stop after two or three minutes.

4. Continue to do this daily, gradually increasing the time of swinging as the child becomes more comfortable. As the time of swinging increases, gradually decrease the amount of support being provided. Encourage the child to hold on to you as you hold the chains on either side of the swing. Eventually, have the child turn around and face in the same direction as you are sitting. The child can then hold on to the chains on the sides of the swing and not on to you.

5. When the child can sit on the swing alone, allow him to do so.

6. When the child is sitting independently on the swing, push him if he needs some help.

7. Teach him to push independently with the directions to "push out with your legs," then "pull in with your arms."

8. The more movement he has created, the more he will want to continue swinging. This gives him a great sense of control and empowerment.

Knee riding

For the small child this is great fun.

1. Allow the child to straddle your knee and give him a "ride."

2. Support him at the hips and back and watch as he exercises the muscles in his back to adjust naturally to an upright and straight position.

3. Gently bounce your knee up and down as much as the child will tolerate.

Exercise balls

These huge inflatable balls are pretty common and not too expensive. If you are lucky enough to have one, it is a great tool for the purpose of helping the child learn where he is in space.

1. Seat the child on the ball facing you.

2. Support him by holding his thighs, hips, or back. Give him enough support so that he feels safe but not confined.

3. If he cannot stay upright with thigh support, hold him by the hips or around the middle (he may have to face away from you for this).

4. Allow him to have a favorite small toy or object in his hands as a distraction. His body will naturally adjust to the balance challenge and his muscles will work to keep him upright. Having a small distraction will also cause the child to be more relaxed and allow his body to do the work. If he is stressed, his mind takes over, and his muscles tighten. This stress hinders the natural balance responses you are hoping to achieve with this activity.

5. Gently and slightly move the ball, front to back, then side to side. As the ball moves you will see him reposition himself so that he stays upright. He will make these adjustments without having to think about it.

6. Always return to the center starting position.

7. Make sure to rest between movements after returning to the starting position.

Movement

Knowing that we are moving and the direction and speed of that movement is another sense that may not develop typically in children with ASDs. They may be overly sensitive to movement or not seem to process it at all. Instinctively understanding how the body is moving develops with experience. The greater the variety of movements a child experiences, the more he is able to understand how he is moving in space. This is a pretty complex system, involving the eyes, inner ear, and brain.

Under leg ball toss

One way to increase the child's awareness and have some fun is the following activity. You will need a small stuffed toy or a soft ball, about five inches (13 cm) in diameter. Have the child give you the ball first over his head, then down between his legs. You give him the ball in return in the opposite manner. If he hands you the ball up above his head, give it back to him down between his legs. This is great fun with a line of friends. If one or two others are available, then the alternating up and down is easier. Once the ball reaches the back of the line, the child with the ball in the back runs to the front and begins the sequence again.

Another alternative to moving the ball "up" and "down" is moving it side to side. The principle of alternation is the same; just pass the object to the right side and then the left side of the person behind.

Touch

Some children with ASDs seem to crave touch and are constantly reaching out and touching all sorts of things. This constant touching may mean that the child is seeking information from the world around him. He is trying to understand objects and people in his immediate vicinity. Or it may mean that he is enjoying the feel of the things he is touching.

Try to detect whether or not the child is touching similar things all the time, if he touches things at certain times, or is touching indiscriminately. If the child is always rubbing or manipulating certain textures or items in his hands, then he is making a clear choice. He is enjoying the feel, and it may be a way that he comforts himself. If, on the other hand, the child does not appear to be choosy about what he touches, he is more than likely using touch as a way to understand the world.

Other children seem not to like touch of any kind. Sometimes a child may strike another child when the other child is within reach. This behavior is often misinterpreted as misbehavior or a violent overture. But if we look at this behavior as a sensory one, then perhaps the child is acting this way as a means to achieve some balance or to understand the world or even to respond to a perceived threat. If the child is not comfortable with being close to others, just standing in line with the class can be a great challenge. If another child is just inches away, but not touching, that may be too close. The child with ASD may be aware of the body heat of his classmate or the static from his clothing. A simple accommodation for school will be to have the child stand at the end of the line. This will allow him to be in line with his classmates, but at the end and at a comfortable distance from the others.

This child does not understand the subtle messages the rest of us understand. The chair does not feel solid enough or the air current from the window or air conditioner is too strong. A child may hit another not out of malice, but simply because he wants information about where he ends and the other person begins.

Another interpretation may be that children with ASDs may not interpret a light or casual touch as just that. It may feel very annoying or even painful. In general we can say that the child is uncomfortable. The goal then is to find balance. Light touch may be relaxing for some and very irritating to others. Paying attention to the sort of touch the child needs and the sort of touch he craves is important. Here are some ideas to promote a balance with the sense of touch for the child. These ideas may be called a "sensory diet." That is, you are providing the child with the sensory experiences he needs to feel more balanced and comfortable in the world.

Compression shirts

These are commercially available. They look like ordinary shirts or may even look like caped costumes or princesses. This clothing provides a steady hug-like feeling all day and tends to comfort the child. A top or bottom made out of this special fabric gives just enough sensory information so that the child is more alert to where he is.

Burrito time

Lay a blanket out on the floor. Fold the blanket two or three times so it is a long and thin shape. Have the child lay on the blanket on the narrow end. Make sure his head is not on the blanket. Roll the child up in the blanket. As he rolls he will be surrounded by layers of material. Children like to pretend they are a burrito or a jelly roll. When they have rolled, using all the material, it is time to unroll. Have the child roll in the opposite direction. This may be repeated two or three times if the child appears to be enjoying the game. The deep pressure from the floor and the compression from the blanket give the child a lot of good information. Soon the child will be holding the end of the blanket by himself as he rolls into a "burrito."

Another good idea if deep pressure or strong touch is what the child craves involves providing a variety of foods. Some foods allow the muscles around the mouth and face to exercise more than others do. Those foods include nuts, granola, carrots, and apples. If the crunchy sounds of these foods disturb the child he can get the same strong feeling from foods such as beef jerky or very dense and chewy breads.

Gentle touch

A light arm stroking can be very relaxing to some. Rubbing along either side of the spine with two fingers can also have a relaxing effect. This can be done while the child is seated or while he is lying on his belly. Applying lotion or sunscreen to arms and face can also become a calming routine before leaving the house in the morning.

Neutral warmth

In general, "neutral warmth" is very calming. This warmth is not too hot and not too cold. The body is so comfortable with this temperature that no adjustments need to be made to maintain balance. Snuggling up under a blanket to read a book or watch television is calming for everyone. Allowing the child to wear his sweatshirt when you think it is too warm outside is an appropriate response to that need for neutral warmth. Unless the child is in danger of becoming overheated to the point of putting his health at risk, allow him his neutral warmth.

Heavy blanket

Another popular item the child may enjoy is a heavy blanket. Even when it is warm outside he might still enjoy the weight of a heavy blanket on the bed. The blanket is providing a lot of information and a secure sense of safety. So, if the child is having some difficulty sleeping or calming down, provide a heavy blanket for him to snuggle under, and see if that makes a difference to his behavior.

Sound

Sound is all around us. We become very skilled at tuning out the unimportant sounds and paying attention to the sounds that we need to or want to hear. Children with ASDs pay attention to all the information that is coming at them, as if it is all equally important. The sound of the dishwasher in the kitchen gets as much attention as the baby brother screaming in the next room and as Mom asking them to pick up their toys. At the same time, cars are zooming down the street, the air conditioner compressor is on and off, and the radio or television is playing. It is no wonder that we often see children with ASDs covering their ears.

Being aware of all that is being asked of the child in terms of understanding the sensory environment is a great step towards helping him to adapt and feel comfortable in the world. Having to experience all the sounds the rest of us can tune out can be a huge challenge to his comfort level. When the child feels comfortable, he will be less likely to pursue behaviors that he uses to self-calm. Those behaviors are often observed in children with ASDs. Some mannerisms include hand flapping, hiding under the furniture, or holding their hands over their ears. We are not saying that these behaviors will completely disappear with the use of a sensory diet, but the sensory diet may help with reducing the child's need for those self-calming behaviors in some situations. Here are some ideas that may work when it is necessary to "turn down the noise."

Turn down the noise

1. Turn off the radio or television when there is no one watching or listening.

2. Make it a rule in the house that if someone wants to speak to another person, that he walk into the room, rather than shout from room to room.

3. Consider using ear plugs or noise canceling headphones, especially in loud public places.

4. Monitor the volume of your own voice and the voices of other people, especially children, in the same room.

5. Be aware of repeating directions or questions. Often children with ASDs need a little more time to understand the spoken word. Allow them that time. If you continue to repeat the same question or statement, it is as though you are continually hitting the "refresh" button on the computer and the child needs to start the process of understanding what is being said over and over again.

Taste

Food provides a variety of sensations besides taste. When we eat we experience temperature, texture, and taste. These characteristics change in the mouth as we chew, suck, and swallow food. Many children on the Autism Spectrum have very specific food preferences. As we move away from the idea that those preferences are not only based on taste, but may also be based on other sensory experiences, we can allow the child to experience other food he may enjoy without much resistance.

For example, perhaps the child enjoys salty and fried food. He may enjoy the feel of the salt as it dissolves, but you are concerned because all the fried food is too fatty and does not provide much nutrition. Find food that may be breaded the same way, but is baked instead. It is true that even the youngest child can tell the difference in brands when his favorite food is being provided under a different label. To avoid this problem, prevent it. It is suggested that you do not get into the habit of always buying the same brand. Being flexible and adapting to change is difficult for many children with ASDs. Providing as many opportunities as possible allows the child to make adaptations daily. This skill is very important in most areas of life.

Having the child with an ASD eat a variety of foods becomes a difficult problem for parents. First, ask yourself what your own food preferences are, and what the rest of the family is eating. Ask yourself if the child is getting balanced nutrition from the food he is eating. By exposing the child to a variety of foods he may find that there are many healthy foods he enjoys. A simple and popular method to know if your child is getting a balanced diet is to look at the color of the food he is eating. Natural colors are what to look for, not artificial color enhancers. If the food diet has greens, reds, yellows, and browns (grains or meats), there is a good chance the diet is balanced.

If you notice that the child enjoys crunchy and salty foods, look for healthy alternatives that provide those elements, although doing so might take some effort. There are recipes available that help concerned parents create seemingly unhealthy foods with healthier ingredients. Using cauliflower instead of white potatoes for mash is one example. The texture of the vegetable when it is boiled and mashed is surprisingly similar to potatoes. The flavor is also similar and will be more so as you add the familiar spices or other ingredients. It may be that the child enjoys the feel of the food, rather than the taste. If that is the case, then the opportunity to substitute healthy alternatives is plentiful. Many children enjoy snack foods that crunch and crumble. Another example of a food texture preference is crunch. Some examples include carrots for crunch or raisins for chewy experiences. Adding some wholegrain rice cakes for the child to crunch and crumble along with his chips may satisfy his crunch need while adding some nutrition. Rice cakes are usually baked and come in a large variety of flavors.

Prevention is much easier than cure, especially when it comes to picky eating. We talk more about ideas to expand the child's eating repertoire in Chapter 5. For now, just keep in mind that a colorful variety of natural foods will more than likely provide a healthy diet for the child.

Smell

The sense of smell is primal. Specific smells can trigger emotions, memories, or cravings.

Some children with ASDs are very sensitive to odors. The same child may say, "You smell like butterflies" one day, and the next tell you that you smell "really bad." In general when living or working or just being with children with ASDs, it is a good idea to keep extraneous fragrances to a minimum. Think of the layers of fragrance a woman may wear in a single day. Bath products have a distinctive fragrance, and then add deodorant, hair products, makeup, perfume, and laundry products. One woman can be a walking fragrance bouquet.

If the child is having trouble sleeping, participating in bathing, or even getting dressed, it might be that the fragrance associated with the activity is the problem. Perhaps the sheets or clothing are washed with a fragrant detergent, or the shampoo or soap has a strong scent. If you suspect that this may be the cause of some discomfort for the child, use unscented products. That being said, we cannot possibly live in a fragrance-free world.

Getting used to unpleasant odors is something that the child can learn. There are times when odors cannot be prevented and should not be. If you are a coffee drinker, the child will need to get used to that strong aroma in the morning. Or the child may not like the cooking odors emanating from your latest culinary masterpiece. Here are some ideas that can be tried with a child of any age. Do not change your odor-causing behavior. Instead try the following.

1. Explain to the child in advance that he will be exposed to an odor that in the past he has found to be unpleasant. If explaining does not work, then proceed with the following suggestion.

2. Tell the child that the odor will exist, and the approximate amount of time he may expect the odor to be in his world. Use gestures such as pointing to the clock or a picture of his favorite pasta sauce to give the child more information in a way that he can understand.

3. Save a special toy or activity that you know the child especially enjoys for this time. Let the child know he may engage in that special activity at the same time the odor may be present. For example, you can allow him to read his favorite book or watch his favorite video close to or in the kitchen as dinner is being prepared. This begins to associate a positive experience with the odor. The child may be so interested in his favorite pastime that the odor may no longer be noticed.

4. Do not call attention to the fact that the child is tolerating the once objectionable odor. Give him the non-verbal message that sometimes you expect him to accept things that are not

enjoyed. Starting with simple elements at home can lead to the bigger goal. That is, allowing children with ASDs to be able to participate in the world around them as independently as possible. It is virtually impossible to prevent the child from having experiences he does not enjoy. Teaching him at a young age and in as many different settings as possible will go a long way towards teaching him to adapt to the world.

Vision

Some children with ASDs have very sensitive visual skills. Many are said to be visual learners; that is, children who take in information that is *shown* rather than *stated* to them. They may be more able to learn and retain information this way. Many children with ASDs attend to visual details. They may seem to be staring at nothing at all, when in fact they are looking at how the light is reflecting in the dust that is flying through the air.

Respecting the child's visual skills and unique abilities honors his distinctive makeup. This strength, when directed, can be used to the child's advantage. When choosing clothing for yourself or the child, or when decorating his room, be aware of the visual environment. Too many patterns or clutter may distract the child, and he may not know where to focus his attention. Many children with ASDs pay attention to details without being aware of the whole picture. The child might look at all elements of something without priority, so that the speck of dirt on the table may engage his attention as much as the plate of cookies and glass of milk that is set in front of him. Keep this in mind, and you can begin to understand his world.

It has been reported that children with ASDs can see the subtle and very fast flicker of fluorescent light bulbs. This ability is important to keep in mind as the child begins preschool or school. If the child has some difficulty in the class, one of the reasons could be the lighting.

Other common speed bumps that can occur in a typical classroom regarding vision are objects hanging from the ceiling. These items typically spin in inconsistent patterns due to air currents. This movement can be a very big problem for children with ASDs for many reasons. First, the child may become visually distracted and stop paying attention to the teacher. The spinning of these items is not predictable, and this could cause distress in the child. Children with ASDs feel more comfortable with order and predictability.

Visual tracking, as discussed in Chapter 2, is the smooth movement of the eyes as they follow objects in the environment. Unfortunately, this skill is not usually tested during a simple vision screening. Although tracking does not impact the visual acuity skills, so a child with poor tracking skills can have 20/20 vision, it does influence balance, coordination, and attention. It is very easy to see if the child is visually tracking. Hold a favorite object about three feet (a meter) from the face. See if he follows the object with his eyes only or if he needs to turn his whole body to see it. At home, it is fun to play at tracking by asking the child to follow you or favorite items using just his eyes. Move the objects to be tracked side to side, up and down, in circles, and close and far. Do this for only two or three minutes at a time once per day. If the child understands your directions, ask him to stay still and only use his eyes. If he is unable to do this, or if his eye movement is not smooth, he may have a visual tracking challenge. There are professionals who provide vision therapy for these issues.

Attention

It is easy to understand how the senses described in this chapter can have an impact on attention. If the child does not know where he is in space, he will not feel settled. If the child is feeling unsettled, he will not be able to attend to a story, a teacher, or non-verbal cues from friends.

If the child does not intuitively understand where his body is in relation to the walls, furniture, or other people, he will not be able to understand how to behave in the environment. This is also true if the child is not comfortable with movement, odors, or things he is seeing. He could be spending so much energy trying not to fall or even feeling dizzy that he simply does not have the ability to pay attention to anything else.

If smells in the environment or touch sensations are uncomfortable, learning will be difficult. The child might also not know which visual elements of the environment are important and which are not. He may be paying very close attention to something that is of great interest, and it may not be the most important part of a lesson.

Understanding how children with ASDs experience the world is important. Deciding which sensory experiences to pay attention to is something we all do all day, every day. Children with ASDs need our help to guide them through this process. Using some of the activity ideas presented here are good first steps towards helping the child connect with the world.

Chapter 5

Daily Living Skills

In this chapter we discuss those tasks that we all do every day, and do not really think about. As we go through our morning routine, we are not thinking about our shower while we are under the running water. Perhaps we are thinking about the time, and if the children are ready for school. Or perhaps as we are getting dressed we are composing an email message in our mind, which we plan to send later that day. We go through our routines without much attention to what we are doing, and in some magical way all these many tasks get accomplished.

Children with ASDs must be aware of each step at the time they are engaged in that task. They need to pay attention to what they are doing as they learn these skills. Often, when a child is having difficulty with a task or is slow to learn, it seems much easier just to do it yourself to save time. When you have the urge to do one of these tasks for the child, stop and ask yourself this question, "Do I want to be still doing this for him when he is 18 years old?" If the answer is, "No," then it is worth the time it takes to allow him to do it himself or to teach him to do the task.

Children with ASDs have the ability to do all the tasks we call "daily living skills" or "life skills." They need to learn them at a slower pace but, make no mistake, they can accomplish these tasks successfully. Breaking down each task into a series of very small steps that are practiced over and over is a very effective method to teach complex, multi-step routines. In this chapter we discuss a variety of methods you can use to help the child learn these important independent skills.

As with all skills, it is a good idea to approach teaching from the strengths of the child. Children with ASDs thrive with schedules and routines and are very serious about following rules. These strengths work very well when teaching daily living skills. Providing and maintaining a predictable routine helps keep the child calm. He will know what to expect and the order in which activities occur. Using a schedule that follows the natural course of the day either at home or in school is a very good idea. Do not create a special or unique schedule for the child.

A word of caution: While following a routine is a good idea, getting stuck within a very restricted set of conditions can be a mistake. Use the schedule as a guideline only. The activities we address here are "real life." Every day, different and unpredictable circumstances occur. Follow the schedule that you develop as closely as possible, within reason.

We will provide some ideas that allow, encourage, and teach flexibility within a structure that is comfortable for you and the child. There will always be times when the routine cannot be followed. It is important to tell the child about these changes with as much notice as possible and return to the set routine as soon as you are able.

Mealtimes

Every family has its own unique menu of foods that are eaten with some regularity. This menu is based on personal likes and dislikes, culture, finances, availability, and in some cases, specific nutritional requirements.

Many children with ASDs insist on certain foods, presented in a specific manner, and served on specific dishes. This complicated set of rituals becomes more and more restrictive over time and, therefore, delays growth and impedes overall practical development.

As with anything that you are teaching the child, it is important to know what you are hoping to accomplish. Is the goal of the meal to have all members of the family sit together and share their days, or is the goal to teach table manners? Perhaps the goal is to enjoy the company of classmates at a celebration. Or perhaps it is to have the child eat some nutritious food. At any time, some or all of these may be possible intentions of the meal. When you have a clear idea of what you expect of the experience, it is easier to communicate those expectations to the child.

If you want the child to sit quietly with others when he eats and provide only healthy foods that he is resistant to trying, he may be disruptive. If your response to the disruption is to give the child a food he considers a treat, you are doing yourself and the child a disservice.

When you provide the treat for the sake of quiet, you are rewarding the disruptive behavior and strengthening that behavior.

Take a step back and look at the messages you are sending to the child. If you want him to sit quietly, then first expect him to do so when he is eating a food that he especially enjoys. If the goal is for the child to eat something new and nutritious, then you can expect some disruptive behavior. Choose your intention and communicate that intention clearly. Here are some helpful guidelines.

1. Determine the goal of the meal. Are you hoping to get something nutritious into the child before you race out the door, or are you hoping for a relaxed family dinner?

2. Many families have set places at the table. This is a fine way to provide structure. To encourage flexibility, use different plates, cups, or utensils. Persuade the child to use plates that have different colors, designs, or patterns that might even be different sizes. Provide a variety of drinking options such as cups with or without handles, small or larger ones, using a straw, or drinking directly from his cup. The younger you begin the process of having the child use a variety of dishes, the less likely he will be to form strong attachments to one particular set or dish along with the belief that those are the only dishes he can use to eat.

3. Allow foods to touch each other. The child may have a difficult time if food is not placed on the plate in a specific order, or if two foods touch. Assure the child that this is not a problem, and show him that everyone else is alright with their food touching or "out of order." Remain calm.

4. When the child is old enough, over the age of three, expect him to use a spoon and a fork. Young children will continue to eat many finger foods, but other foods such as macaroni and cheese, apple sauce, yogurt, and pudding should be eaten with a fork or a spoon.

5. Provide the child with the opportunity to try different foods. Many children develop restricted diets and refuse other foods based on color, texture, smell, size, presentation, or taste. Keep trying. If you continue to offer the food and place a very

small amount of that food on the child's plate, he will get the message that trying it is an expectation. Without words, you are communicating that this is a food the family eats, and he is expected to eat it, as well. You may need to do this many more times than you like before the child will taste even the smallest amount, but do not give up.

6. Set a reasonable amount of time you expect the child to remain at the table. If the child is getting most of his nutrition from milk, for example, offer the milk only after he has attempted to eat the other foods you have prepared, within the time you have determined. After the child has made an attempt to try the other foods or has sat for the set time you have determined, then give him his milk. You are showing him that he is able to try new foods or at the very least sit at the table for the set amount of time you find acceptable.

7. Use a timer to avoid power struggles. When a timer is set for the child to see, he will begin to understand that there is an expectation that he will try some food or sit politely for a set period of time. The timer becomes the enforcer of the time frame instead of you. It is as if you and the child are working together to achieve something before the timer sounds. Depending on the child and his tolerance for sitting at the table, the timer may be set for 5 to 20 minutes.

8. If the child has a very restricted diet or you believe he has some food sensitivities, consult your medical professional.

Dressing

The child might have very specific ideas about his clothing. From a young age, you might determine that the child will only wear pants with elastic waistbands or clothing without labels. These preferences are related to touch sensitivity. Chapter 4 talks about various touch or feeling preferences the child may have. Here we discuss the actual process of dressing and methods to teach this skill to the child, so he will become independent when he dresses each day.

What's the weather?

The child may have certain items of clothing that he loves to wear. He may wear a long-sleeved hooded sweatshirt even when the summer sun is blazing. Or he may insist on wearing only a thin t-shirt when it is snowing. Teaching the child at a young age to dress according to the weather will help him as he gets older. This will start him on the way to making healthy decisions.

With the child in the room, look out the window. If it is raining or snowing say, "Wow, it is wet (or cold) outside—I'd better wear clothes that will keep me warm. Let's find something to keep you warm and dry too." You can open the window to feel a few drops of rain, the cold air, or the hot summer sun. Have the child experience the weather, as well. Few words are needed for the child to understand that he feels wet, cold, or hot.

This discussion will offer the child several ways to understand what the weather is like outside. He will hear your explanation, see the parts of the environment that you are talking about, and feel the cold, wet, or heat for himself.

Let's pick

Getting the child involved in the process of choosing his clothing each day and teaching him how this is done gives him a sense of personal responsibility. Choosing clothes can be done with children as young as three years old. Use one word or phrase for each item beginning with underwear, and gather each article of clothing in the order it will be put on. Saying, "Blue undies, white t-shirt, white socks," for example, helps the child pay attention to each item of clothing. Being quiet and only speaking a few words at a time will help the child concentrate on getting dressed rather than trying to understand the extra words you are saying.

As the child gets older and expresses an interest in taking his own clothing from his dresser, by all means, encourage him to do so! Reinforce his independence with a few words, a smile, and nod of approval. For example, you can say, "Great, warm shirt for a cold day."

Getting into clothes

Teaching the child actually to put his clothing on can be an overwhelming task, but it does not need to be. Just take a deep breath and break the dressing down into very small tasks. Often a child will learn to take off his clothing before he learns to put it on. Encourage him to do this, at the right time. As he undresses, he is learning how the clothing feels coming off and which items cover which parts of his body. When you are teaching the child to dress, do not rush. Rushing will communicate stress and feeling stressed decreases the child's chances of learning. If you do not have the time to feel patient as the child is dressing, then save the teaching for a later date. Just make sure to take the time to put some effort into this skill at least three times a week.

To begin the process of teaching the child to dress, start with the most simple items first. Socks are usually tight, and require a certain amount of precision to get them on correctly. A short-sleeved or sleeveless undershirt may be easier as a starting item. Even putting on an undershirt is a task with multiple steps. To start, see if the child can slip his head through the neck opening and then you can help him with putting his arms in to the sleeves. If he starts to put his arms in first, let him. Then you can support his effort as his head goes in next. There are no laws about the order clothing is put on! Allow the child to develop his own style as long as he gets the job done.

After the clothing item is on, smooth it down against his body. Use the kind of touch (firm or gentle) you determine is enjoyable for the child. Smile and do not use too many words. These few seconds can be very important in communicating that he has accomplished putting on his shirt. This additional touch will confirm that he has accomplished a meaningful task. After all the chosen clothing items are on, smile and tell him how wonderful he looks. Allow yourself a moment of pride and know that you are on your way to helping the child become an independent person.

What about style?

Fashion and a sense of style are personal expressions. Children with ASDs often have strong opinions about color, fabric, and design. More often than not the child's sense of style will not be the same as yours.

When this happens, you need to ask yourself again what is important. If you are on your way to a formal family dinner and you want the child to look a specific way, then planning is important. We will discuss these special circumstances later in Chapter 6, when we look at getting prepared for special events. For daily dressing, allow the child to express himself. If the child attends a school with a specific dress code or uniform, the child must comply with this restriction. Allow the child self-expressive dress during the weekends and after school. Changing from a school uniform to clothing in which the child feels more comfortable is a good transition. Changing to his choice of clothing demonstrates to him, without words, that he is home now.

Grooming

Like it or not, people who do not know us use appearance to form opinions about us and about our children. Grooming is also an important part of maintaining one's health. If the child is not happy about all the intrusive activities that are part of looking good, you have a challenge. Take heart! We will give you some guidelines that can help make these activities easier. The first thing to remember is that children with ASDs will learn well from imitation. If he can watch you shower (for example), he will have an easier time understanding what is expected during this process.

The specific tasks we are talking about are using the bathroom, hand washing, nail care, bathing (or showering), hair combing, teeth brushing, and nose blowing. As with all self-care activities, the earlier your child gets involved and participates in taking care of his needs, the more likely he will feel comfortable and become independent.

Bathroom

While we will not discuss the specifics of potty training here, there are some issues that can be addressed specifically for children with ASDs.

1. The child learns by watching. Disregard any of your own feelings of embarrassment and allow the child to observe while you use the toilet. Explain and demonstrate how you are moving and touching your body and using the paper, for

example. Make sure he is able to observe every step of the process. Do not assume that the child understands what is happening when your hand is out of sight. Showing rather than telling is very important in his learning process.

2.   The noise of the flushing sound can disturb the child. If this is the case, close the lid prior to flushing. This will dull some of the sound, but not eliminate it. If the noise is still a problem, wait until the child is out of the room to flush. He can learn to flush later on when he is older and fully toilet trained.

3.   When teaching the child to clean himself with paper, make sure to give him enough so that his hand is covered. You can wrap the paper around his hand. This avoids any problems if the child has not yet developed hand dexterity. He can use his entire hand and be successful.

4.   Make sure he has done a complete job, with a quick follow-up using a moist wipe.

Hand washing

Hand washing is the most effective and important way for the child to stay healthy. Follow these steps, one at a time. If the child shows that he can complete the first or last step, help him with the others until he is able to complete the routine.

1.   Turn on the water.

2.   Use one pump of preferred liquid hand soap. You can use the same soap you use in the shower in a small pump dispenser placed next to the sink. Using the same soap provides some connection to bath time and provides that comforting continuity. If the child is sensitive to different textures or fragrances, using the same soap is important. Each brand of liquid soap feels different. When you find the one that is acceptable to the child, stick with it.

3.   Place the child's hands under running water for just a moment to add water to the soap. Sing the alphabet song or another song as the child soaps his hands. Help him to soap his hands only if he needs the help. Rub first the front then the backs

of his hands all the way up to the wrists, making lots of suds. Make sure he soaps the backs, palms, in between fingers, and fingertips. Placing the five fingers of one hand into the palm of the other, then reversing, will keep the nails and fingertips clean.

4.   After the song is over, have the child hold his hands under the running water and gently rub until all the soap is gone. Turn off the water.

5.   Use the towel that is right next to the sink to dry his hands. Make sure the child dries between his fingers. Only provide help along the way that is necessary.

Nail care

It is very important to keep the child's nails clean. Dirt under the fingernails contains many germs that can easily be ingested when eating finger foods.

1.   Keep the child's nails as short as possible.

2.   Use a large clipper so each nail may be done with one clip, rather than a series of smaller clips. The feeling against sensitive fingertips and the sound may be disturbing to the child.

3.   Clip finger and toenails soon after a bath, when they are the softest.

4.   If dirt is collecting under the fingernails, use a soft nail brush. Some nail brushes have suction cups so they can be attached to the inside of the sink. This is a way that nails can be cleaned one hand at a time without the need for the opposite hand to help. This is an especially good idea for children who have some trouble using both hands together in a coordinated way. This interesting item may be just the thing that intrigues the child and encourages him to use it.

Bath time

After some trial and error, you have discovered the water temperature that the child prefers.

1. Run the bath at the preferred temperature. Using a liquid soap eliminates the need to lather from a hard dry bar of soap. Liquid soap also prevents the common problem of dropping the soap in the middle of the shower.

2. Use a soft or rough textured cloth, depending on the child's preference.

3. Apply enough liquid soap to the cloth so that it will last for the entire bath or shower. Find a soap that is fragrance free if the child is sensitive to smells. Lavender or vanilla fragrances are calming, however, and if the child enjoys these, they can be used at bedtime to promote sleep. Mint fragrances are energizing and are good to use in the morning if the child has a difficult time waking up and moving.

4. Start with the child's face, avoiding his eyes. Scrub from top to bottom. Do not rush.

5. If he is reaching for the cloth, allow him to wash any parts that he is interested in washing.

6. Wash his hair last as he will not feel cold from his wet head while the rest of his body is being scrubbed. There are many products that combine shampoo and conditioner. Use a combination product to eliminate a step to simplify the bathing process.

7. Rinse from head to toe and you are done!

8. Wrap the child in a large robe or towel to cover his entire body, including his head. This will get the job done quickly and prevent the cold air from disturbing him.

9. This is now a great time to rub some soothing lotion or oil on the child if his bath is at night. If bath time is in the morning, then it is a good time to use sunscreen. Many products for children are fragrance free.

Taking care of belongings

Here is another area of life where children with ASDs benefit from rules and order. Learning to care for toys and other belongings is an important part of growing up. Small children are capable of participating. The old saying, "A place for everything and everything in its place" holds very true for these children. Here are some basics to consider that will help the child be successful caring for his belongings.

1. At the end of the day, have an easily reachable spot for the child to place his dirty laundry. An open basket is easier than one with a lid for your small child to use. Not having to open a lid, but simply placing items into a large opening will provide a successful experience that is important and encourages involvement in the process.

2. Placing a series of low hooks near the entry door is an excellent way to communicate to the child the proper place to hang his jacket when he gets home.

3. Have a visually clear place for categories of items. Books go on the bookshelf and trucks in the truck bin and so on.

4. After an activity or playtime ends, allow for a specific "cleanup" time. For instance, if the child has 30 minutes to play before dinner, after 20 minutes have passed tell him that he has five more minutes until cleanup time. Then, five minutes later, help him to begin the process of cleaning up. Of course, messy activities require a longer time to clean up and store items, but putting a book away will take less than one minute. No matter the activity or the time required, reinforce the cleanup period. This will serve as a good transition period, and develop a healthy behavior pattern.

5. Provide space. It is much more pleasant to put a book on a shelf or blocks in a bin when there is plenty of room for the items to fit. Having to squeeze something in to make it fit requires a lot of planning that the child might not understand. It also causes stress and a sense of urgency that decreases the child's willingness to participate in the cleanup at all.

6.   A gentle approach is important, especially with some complex technology that children commonly use. Show the child how to use special care when looking after technology. Set the child up for success by giving him the use of items that can withstand his style of touch. Allow the child to observe how you care for and maintain more fragile things. When he is ready to participate in cleaning and charging devices so they are ready for the next day, allow him to help.

7.   Less is definitely more. Children with ASDs are easily overwhelmed and distracted by too many choices and too many items. Limit duplications and keep things simple. Clear spaces promote calm feelings.

8.   Very small children, as young as three years old, are capable of cleaning up mess. They may not do an excellent job, but allowing the child to start the process of wiping up milk, for example, initiates the learning process. Participating in cleaning up also provides children with a sense of responsibility and understanding of consequences.

Often the term "consequences" is used in a negative way. Consequences are simply the natural results of behavior. So, if there is a drip of milk on the table as someone pours, the natural consequence will be the need to wipe it up. This is not a bad thing, just a normal part of drinking a glass of milk.

If the child is not happy about all the intrusive activities that go in to looking good, you have a challenge. Take heart! We will give you some guidelines that can help make these activities easier.

Daily schedules

Having a daily and weekly schedule is hugely important for children with ASDs. A schedule provides a feeling of security, predictability, and safety. The child needs to know what to expect and when to expect it. Arranging the day for the child in a sequential manner will allow you and the child to feel more comfortable. Following these suggestions can help.

Make sure to include time in the child's schedule for him to be alone. If he wants to use this time to flap his hands or make noises, he may do this during this time. The child may be working hard all day to control noises or movements that others do not want to see or hear and he does not want to share. He needs some time to be allowed to engage in these behaviors. Let him move or make noises in ways he chooses, but provide him with the appropriate places and times. Give him 30 minutes a day for this activity. You can call it "Johnny's Time," for example.

Keep the child informed about what will happen during the day. Before the child is able to read, use a visual schedule. Many children with ASDs, even if they do speak, may respond better to visual instructions than to spoken words.

Visual schedules

A visual schedule can be created in this manner:

1. Take photos of the child doing certain things, such as eating or brushing his teeth. Or you can cut out magazine pictures to represent activities. Create cards approximately one to two inches square (2.5 to 5 cm) for each activity picture. Many typical daily activity pictures can be found on the internet.

2. Attach a small piece of Velcro or sticky tack to the back of each picture.

3. Place each picture on a larger board or in pages of a binder in the order that the tasks are to be completed.

4. As each activity is finished, remove the picture to the designated "done" space on the bottom of the big schedule or in the back of the book. An envelope with the word "DONE" can also be created to hold the pictures of completed activities.

5. Encourage the child to point to each activity before starting. When the activity or experience is completed, have the child help you move the picture and point out the next part of his day.

6. As the child learns to read, exchange the pictures for words. This can be a lifelong way for the child to organize his time. Many adults use lists to keep them on track as the day progresses.

Keeping organized

One of the kindest things you can do for children with ASDs is to maintain as much organization as possible. Staying organized can be a huge challenge, but a little planning goes a long way. Find one time during the week when you can plan the essentials, such as laundry and grocery shopping. If in a school setting, the necessary accommodations need to be planned for each lesson.

Place all these events, requirements, expectations, and any special appointments on the weekly or daily calendar. Alert the child to these events at the start of each day. Allow yourself the luxury of this time to plan and you will thank yourself later. Be kind to yourself and schedule in times when you can regroup and recharge. When you take good care of yourself, you are better able to care for the child.

Sleep

Sleep may be a challenge for children with ASDs. As you become aware of the various activities the child enjoys that help him feel comfortable, sleep can become easier. The goal is to have the child learn some techniques that teach him to calm himself so that he will go to sleep on his own. It is never too early for the child to learn to be self-sufficient. Here are some guidelines to follow:

1. Turn off the television, videos, or computers 30 minutes to an hour before bedtime. The light from these screens interferes with the natural preparation the child's body engages in to encourage sleep.

2. Warmth is often calming. We have discussed neutral warmth and the calming feeling it promotes that is especially useful when trying to fall asleep. The child might also enjoy a quilt that has some weight to it. Allow him to use a heavier quilt even during warm weather.

3. Lavender or vanilla scents can calm the child if he enjoys these fragrances.

4. Keeping a bedtime routine will communicate to the child and his body that it is time for sleep. A typical routine may be: bath, story, lights out.

5. The child may like to have you lay beside him as he falls asleep. Perhaps he enjoys having you rub his head or his back with slow smooth movements. This is fine at times. Just keep in mind that you do not want the child to become too dependent on you to fall asleep.

6. Progressive relaxation is a method that many individuals of all ages find helpful. Children with ASDs can especially enjoy the sequential nature of this suggestion. Simply tell the child to tense or "make tight" different parts of his body, then allow the tense part to feel "loose and relaxed." Progress from the toes to the nose or from the head to the toes as you tell the child to tense and relax the parts of his body. Have him hold the muscles tight for a slow count of five. The progression can be as follows: face, arms, tummy, then legs. With an older child, the body parts can be separated into smaller segments. This progressive tightening and releasing naturally allows the child to feel relaxed and tired. After a while the child can perform this sequence without your direction. Independence is the goal.

7. Using the same sleep and wake times, even on the weekends (the child's body does not know the different days of the week) helps the child reinforce his sleep/awake cycle. His body needs to get at least eight to ten hours of sleep every night. Making sure that the bedtime routine starts one hour before lights out is important. Lights out should be at least eight to ten hours before the child needs to wake up. For example, if the child needs to wake up at 6 am to allow for a non-rushed morning routine, then the bedtime routine needs to start between 7 and 8 pm in order for the child to get ten hours of sleep.

Chores

As with taking care of his belongings, the very young child can have some simple chores. This participation allows him to feel a part of the family, group, or class and communicate that sense of belonging. This is so even if he does not have the words to understand. Begin when he is as young as three. Your three-year-old may be capable of putting laundry or toys in a designated basket. He can also carry spoons to the table or put glue sticks out for others to use. Think of other simple tasks that the family or group does daily. Assign the child a job and make it part of his visual schedule. Expect him to do this every day, and increase his chores and responsibilities as he grows.

Chapter 6

Activities in the Home, School, and Community

Play

It is the job of all children to play. Through play they learn about the world, how things work, their bodies, and relationships. Communication and social interactions are great challenges for children with ASDs. Many children with ASDs develop special interests, and these special interests often provide years of pleasure and fulfillment for people with an ASD. While the special interest of the child should not be discouraged, broadening his horizons is a good idea. This involvement in subjects and experiences outside of his special interest provides more opportunities for learning than if the child continues to be involved with a limited number of subjects.

The child may need encouragement to play with toys, textures, or people outside his comfort zone or apart from his special interest. Below are some ideas that work to slowly involve the child in new play. These activities allow him to learn and develop new skills.

Playing alone

Children with ASDs play alone even when others are available as play companions. This tendency is not a problem by itself, at times, but does not afford the child opportunities to develop social and communication skills. Play is the time where these relationship skills are developed and practiced in childhood. It is during play that the child will try various roles, learn how to relate with others, and work to make others understand him.

While these skills may not be priorities for the young child with an ASD, interacting with others becomes important as he grows and cares about being understood by others. Play is a safe and wonderful place to begin to encourage the development of the child. Allow the child time each day to play alone, and then enter his world gradually. Playing alongside the child is called "parallel play."

Parallel play

Parallel play occurs when two children play close to each other, but are not interacting. Most young children engage in parallel play at some time, but not always. Children with ASDs may be content to play alone all the time. The activities suggested here encourage communication and build social skills during play. If, for example, the child is building with LEGO™, start to build with LEGO™ as well. Share the supply of building blocks that the child is using. If he is constructing something that is not too complicated, copy it. This may get his attention, and even a smile. He will notice that you have created a similar structure.

By copying his project you are communicating to him that he is building something worthy of being copied. You are noticing what he is making. He is making an impact in the world and you see it and understand it. The goal is to allow the child the joy of playing while gradually and slowly letting him know that he is communicating with you and you are seeing and understanding him. The next step in using play to encourage communication is to play with the child.

Playing together

Many children with ASDs use their vision to understand the world. The visual skills and sharp attention to visual detail is a great strength for these children. Encourage increased social interaction during play with the use of these visual skills.

"ROLY POLY": ONE OF THE FIRST GAMES A BABY LEARNS

When you think about the skills involved in this game, it does not seem so childish. To play this game, the child needs to understand turn taking, watching the ball, and waiting for the right moment to roll it back to you.

1. Encourage this game by using a ball with contrasting colors, such as black and white stripes, or a ball that has some glitter in it. Any ball that is visually interesting works.

2. Begin by sitting very close, on the floor, and facing the child. Then roll the ball to him.

3. WAIT.

4. Observe what the child does.

5. If the child touches the ball at all, this is a great beginning.

6. Allow the child to move the ball in any direction.

7. When the ball is away from the child's hands, roll it back to him.

8. If the child does not touch the ball at all, then move the ball back to the child's space, and roll it away from him. Demonstrate to the child the action he is to make.

9. Be patient.

10. Once you have repeated this a number of times, the child will begin to touch the ball and attempt to move it.

11. Minimize your speaking. Avoid exclamations such as, "That's great!" A smile and the return of the ball is what the child needs to understand and to continue the activity.

Another way to encourage playing together is to use the same materials the child is using. If he is building, watch him for a while then add to his structure with another block. If the child is lining up cars or trucks, take one of those vehicles and pretend it is going for a ride. Making the appropriate motor sounds gives the child the idea that his cars and trucks can be used for going on a trip or visiting the garage. His vehicles do more than just get in line. Demonstration is a very powerful teaching tool. Show the child how to have fun and play with the toys that interest him.

PLAYING WITH SIBLINGS

Younger or older siblings are natural playmates for children with ASDs. Allow the child to develop his own communication style and relationships. Give the child's sibling the opportunity to help. Explain the special ways the child with ASD communicates and the reasons for some of his behaviors.

Be careful not to enlist another sibling as your helper only, and be aware if a parent is becoming too dependent on another child for the care or communication of the sibling with an ASD. Allow the typically developing siblings to play and have their own childhoods. Watching a brother or sister behave naturally is one of the best ways that children with ASDs can learn typical behavior.

PLAY DATES

Many communities have support groups where parents can meet with others who have children with ASDs. These parents share ideas and comfort. Groups such as these provide a great source for friends and play dates. The parents understand the need for structure and some of the challenges the child has with new individuals.

When arranging a play date with a family that does not have children with ASDs, here are some thoughts you may want to share.

1. The child does best when he knows what to expect. If they have a new puppy that will unexpectedly jump, the child needs to know in advance about this possibility.

2. The child may become overwhelmed with too much activity at once. If the plan is to play with LEGO™, then the television should not be on in the background.

3. The child may not enjoy loud noises or strong fragrances.

4. The child may not look at his host or other adults when they are speaking. Explain that the child is not being rude. He is a better listener when he does not have to look directly at the person speaking. They should not take this lack of eye contact personally.

5. When you have a new friend over to your home, explain the concept of sharing to your child. Decide with the child what he will be comfortable having his new friend touch, and decide which games and toys are off limits.

6. Set the first play date for a short period of time. The duration should be no longer than one hour or shorter, so that the playtime ends before the children get tired. Ending the date with the child wanting to spend more time with his new friends encourages another date. This next date is anticipated with a positive feeling and can be the source of great learning opportunities, especially social competencies.

Breaks at school

Once the child begins school, he will be expected to be away from home for hours at a time. Make clear to the child's teacher the experiences that tend to overwhelm the child. Some of these things might include noises, smells, touch, or being too close to other students.

Explain to the teacher that the child needs to have the opportunity for some time to calm down if the situation in the classroom gets too difficult for him to maintain his behavior in an acceptable manner. Schools provide accommodations for children with special needs.

Identify the behaviors in which the child engages if he is getting anxious so the teacher can anticipate it and be prepared. If the child flaps his hands or makes a noise, runs away, or covers his ears when he is stressed then his teacher needs to know this is a sign. Before the first day of school, arrange a place in the class or school for the child to have as a retreat. If at all possible, bring the child to the class before the first day. He will then have the opportunity to meet the teacher and see the place he can retreat to if the need arises.

Often a corner of a typical class can be set aside with dividers. This space should have limited items of interest; perhaps a bean bag chair and some nice items to touch will be enough. These items may include a very small stuffed animal, a windup toy, or a small car. It is a good idea if each item is small enough to fit into the child's hand. Each toy should have a different feel when touched. Create a plan with the child's teacher that is acceptable to the running of the classroom, can be implemented without disruption, and allows the child time to calm down so he can return to the class routine in the shortest amount of time.

We all need breaks. Teaching the child to know when he needs a break to feel calm is an important part of life. When the child is able to take a break before he has an all-out tantrum, his school success is more likely.

Computer use, television, and videogames

Children need to run and skip, throw and catch, and just *move* for their bodies and minds to develop. When the child spends time sitting in front of a screen he is not exercising his body. Make sure the child spends at least one hour or more per day in physical exercise. Climbing, running, and swinging help develop his muscles and his mind. Strong muscles allow him to feel calmer and be more successful in school. Believe it or not, strong stomach muscles relate to good handwriting!

Technology

As we write this book, technology is changing at an incredible pace. Children with ASDs may have an uncanny understanding of the newest advances in technology. Technology may be used in many ways to help the child plan his day, organize his tasks, and communicate. Even so, these tools are not the same as person-to-person interaction. Limit the child's use of computers and other impersonal tools to no more than one to one-and-a-half hours per day when he is using them just for fun. If the child is using a piece of technology for school or as an augmentative communication device, then by all means have him use it as appropriate.

Children with ASDs are fortunate to live in a time when there is a lot of technology in common use. Many of these tools that can be seen almost anyplace help the child with an ASD a great deal. One of the most common tools that is gaining in popularity is a hand-held device with a touch screen, such as the iPad and tablet-like devices. These devices appear multiple times in a variety of literature explaining the wide range of uses for the child with an ASD. They often have a "universal design." These design elements include flexibility, simplicity, perception, error tolerance, low physical effort and size, and space appropriateness. They are basically easy to use, and very forgiving of mistakes or clumsiness. At times they seem to understand the intention of the user and make appropriate corrections.

Some devices weigh little more than two pounds (1 kg). They are commonly used by people from all walks of life and easily fit into a student backpack. Very little effort is needed to use a touch screen. The size of the screen and the pictures that need to be touched may compensate for poor motor planning or delayed fine motor dexterity that many children with ASDs display.

In contrast to the "talkers" that are commonly used by children with expressive language delays, the price of a computer tablet is lower, and it weighs less, making it much more available to more people. Someone with an ASD of any age using this technology would not look any different than another person using a tablet. This will go a long way to cutting down on some of the stigma associated with having an expressive language delay.

There are many applications that can be found that can help in this area. The applications may not have been specifically developed as a clinical tool, but are quickly becoming invaluable to parents and children alike. Ask your child's speech therapist to help filter out some useful tools if you decide to get a tablet device.

Worship

At some point in the life of the child, he will possibly find that he is sitting in a house of worship. If this is a regular occurrence, he will have more opportunities to learn how to behave in this setting and increase his capability of proper behavior. If this worship experience is a rare occasion, then more planning is needed. No matter how often the child is in a house of worship, he will probably need to sit quietly, which may be very difficult for the child.

There will be unfamiliar and often hard seats on which to sit. There will be many people he does not know around. The child will be seeing unfamiliar sights and smell all sorts of odors. Here are some ideas that can help you and the child in this situation.

1. Make sure to include the occasion of worship on the child's schedule.

2. If at all possible, take the child for a visit to the building or room prior to the day of worship.

3. Have the child sit on the seat and look around at the different walls, windows, and other distinct characteristics that are only seen in this place. Ask him to identify shapes or images.

4. Explain to the child that when he goes (on whichever day the worship is) there will be many people, and lots of different sounds and smells.

5. Allow the child to bring an item of calming comfort with him. For example, a book he enjoys and is familiar with might be comforting, or any small toy that is quiet and he can play with in his hands without disturbing those around.

6. If he needs to wear unfamiliar clothing, allow him to wear his special outfit a few days before he needs to attend the worship. Doing so gives him a chance to adjust to the new clothing. Allow the child to wear these clothes for play for a few hours. If the clothing remains clean, resist the urge to wash and press the outfit. Do not underestimate the comfort the child will get from putting on clothing that he has previously worn. The clothing will have his scent and already be "broken in." This familiarity will provide comfort to the child during an unfamiliar experience.

7. If the child is required to participate in a ceremony, rehearsal is key. If the child can experience some or all of the sights, sounds, and touches prior to the big day, then he will be prepared. Seeing how he responds during the rehearsal of this important occasion will allow you and the child to be prepared for the experience.

Holidays

Holidays bring changes to our routines that most of us enjoy. The child with ASD may have a different opinion. Just as he is thriving on his regular bedtime and schedule, along comes a holiday. You may believe that all your hard work to keep life organized will come to an end. This does not have to be the case. The child will smell different odors coming from the kitchen as special holiday dishes are prepared, for example. People who do not usually come to visit may be in your home for short stays or days on end. The structured days of school and other activities are disrupted.

Once again, a little planning goes a long way. Remember to:

1. Think about what is really important about the holiday for you and your family.

2. Involve the child in the planning as much as possible.

3. Let the child know that changes are coming by preparing his schedule in advance and showing him the changes. Decrease as many unexpected experiences as possible with these warnings.

4. Keep as much as possible the familiar routines of bedtime, dressing, and morning routines.

5. Encourage the child to participate in any special preparations as much as he wants. He may surprise you by wanting to show his decorations or food creations at special times of the year. This will certainly help him feel a part of the celebrations that everyone else is enjoying.

6. Relax!

Restaurants

Eating meals out in a public place is part of family life. Waiting for food and being in unfamiliar places presents a challenge to many children with ASDs. However, dining out can be done, and happily!

1. Plan with a picture or symbol of the restaurant placed on the child's schedule.

2. Look up the menu and decide in advance the best choice for the child. If at all possible involve the child in the process of choosing what he will order or what will be ordered for him.

3. If you think there will be a delay before the food arrives, allow the child to have a snack so he is not too hungry before the meal arrives.

4. Plan the restaurant meal as close as possible to the time the child usually eats this meal at home.

5. Arrive at the restaurant prepared with quiet activities that you know the child enjoys and that will keep him seated even if he is not eating. This preparation gives the rest of the family a chance to enjoy their meals.

If you know that the child has a difficult time with strong odors or loud noises, avoid these places. If you cannot avoid them, use the strategies you will discover in the next chapter on calming techniques to help keep the outing progressing in order and calm.

Running errands with the family

The list of chores that have to get done seems to get longer all the time. At times it may be unavoidable to take the child out of the comfort of his routine to get all the needs of the family met. There may be a lot of getting into and out of the car. Or you may use public transportation to get around town. During these times, it is important that the child understands what is happening. Explain where you are going and what it may be like for the child. He may need to get out of the car for just a moment to pick something up with you. Or he may need to be quiet and wait as an older sibling finishes an event at school such as a sports practice or Scouts.

Prepare the child as much as possible. Make sure he is as rested as possible, not hungry, and does not need to use the bathroom before the outing. Participating in family activities, even short errands, are part of family life. Allowing the child to experience these changes to routines is a great learning experience. He is part of the family and an active member of that family. You are not doing the child a favor if you protect him from every little bump in the road. Leaving the child at home with a babysitter can isolate him and cause him to feel more separate than perhaps he already does. Whenever possible bring him along. How will he ever learn how to deal with all the unexpected things that arise in life if he never learns that these events are safe and harmless?

Allowing the child to bring his favorite items on these errands provides some sense of comfort and control in an otherwise unpredictable situation. Those items may include a favorite snack, a book, or hand-held game.

Leisure

Children with ASDs may seem to have a different idea of recreation than you. It may seem to you that he really enjoys sitting at the window and watching the light change. If this is something he does enjoy, then by all means allow him his staring, but in limited amounts in the appropriate places and times.

Learning to be in public, enjoying what the world has to offer, and participating in those things is an important part of growing up for the young child with an ASD. Here are some common activities, along with accommodations that will help to make those experiences more pleasant.

Going to the movies

There are so many wonderful movies for children that are best viewed in a theater with other children. Movies can be very loud; theaters can have strong odors, and be dark. These elements may cause some difficulties for the child.

To decrease the sound volume, allow the child to wear noise canceling headphones. You can purchase disposable ear plugs that reduce noise as well. Sitting near the back of the theater will provide more light and lessen the need to walk in the dark to find a seat.

Some movie theaters now offer special "sensory friendly" showings of popular children's movies. These special showings have brighter lights, lower volume, and tolerate the need for children to move or call out during the show. Call your local theater for information and a schedule for this wonderful opportunity.

As far as the strong smell of popcorn goes, perhaps it will encourage the child to try a new food. Make sure you bring along a snack; everyone enjoys snacking in the movies!

Bicycle riding

Bicycle riding has been a family favorite for hundreds of years. The exercise is wonderful, as is the fresh air. As the child learns to pedal, and develops the skill to ride a two-wheeler, make sure he is wearing a helmet. This is a habit that should be developed from the first time he rides—the child should begin wearing a helmet when he is on a tricycle.

Develop a routine that the child can follow that includes safety and taking care of his bicycle. Providing a place for his bicycle and helmet that is easy for him to reach is very important and encourages independence. If he can wheel his bicycle out to the street without help, he will gain a sense of confidence and pride. After the ride, show the child the proper way to put his bicycle away. Perhaps it got dusty or muddy. Show him the best way to wipe it down so that it remains in good condition and it is ready for the next ride. If he is old enough to ride, he is old enough to take care of his bicycle.

Bowling and arcades

Going to a bowling alley or a games arcade are very popular family outings. Children with ASDs may have a difficult time enjoying these places, however, because of all that happens there. These places are very noisy, with balls knocking down pins, lights flashing, and games making all sorts of noises. Of course there are all the other noises the many children are making too. The child may become overwhelmed. If going to these places is something that your family enjoys and you would like your child with ASD to enjoy as well, try these suggestions.

1. Travel to the arcade with another adult.

2. Prepare the child in advance by telling him he is going somewhere very loud and noisy.

3. Allow him to bring his comfort items (a favorite stuffed toy, etc.).

4. Make an agreement with him that he will stay for a certain amount of time, then take a break to go outside with the other adult for some quiet time.

5. Encourage the child to participate in small increments. Perhaps he can roll one or two bowling balls, or watch the arcade games and the other children play for one to two

minutes at a time, initially. Show him the passing of time on your watch. Keep to the agreement of the time frames.

6. He may want these quiet breaks during many visits to the arcade, then one day decide he wants to experience more.

7. If at the agreed upon time he appears to be having a good time, remind him that he can take a break if he wants.

8. Let him decide if he needs a break or not. If he says he does not need a break at that time, then reset the time for another two or three minutes.

9. If you have asked him three times if he needs a break, smile. A milestone has been reached. Tell him that he can take a break when he needs one, and leave it to him to let you know when that time comes.

The important lesson that the child will learn is that he is the one who decides when an experience is overwhelming for him and when he needs a break. This is a wonderful lifelong lesson.

Chapter 7

Calming Techniques

Being proactive is the best way for the child to remain calm. This is true for children with ASDs as well as those who love and care for them. Learning takes place in a calm setting. Being prepared saves time and frustration for all involved. A stressful time is not the time to practice a calming technique. If the child has learned a calming technique, the stressful time is a good time to remind him that he has a tool he can use.

Skills become part of one's selection of behaviors when the efforts to develop those skills are rewarded. The rewards that have the greatest effect and are the most lasting are the rewards that come from within. When a child is learning to walk, the mere act of standing up and getting to where he wants to go, without falling, is reinforcing. No one has to give him a sticker for taking a few steps. He keeps working at it because it feels good to accomplish this task.

This intrinsic reinforcement is true for most skills, especially self-calming. When the reward comes from the activity itself, it is more likely that the child will do the activity when he needs to feel calmer. He feels good because of what he can accomplish and will repeat the task. With repetition comes improved skill. As he is learning, the child will need support in the form of time to practice the skills. He also needs support in using the skills at the right time. A little reminder, even in the form of the adult taking a deep breath in view of the child, can be all that is needed for the child to do so as well.

Parents and carers need to have a delicate balance when it comes to helping the child remain calm. On the one hand, you do not want him to be very upset or have a tantrum. On the other hand, he must learn to experience feeling upset and learn to calm himself before the problem escalates. Continually protecting the child from unpleasantness will not teach him to cope.

Staying calm at home

We have talked about providing a predictable routine and schedule for the child. This is a fundamental way to help keep calm for you and the child. There are many ways to provide a set routine if a visual schedule does not work for your family. You can use a clock and have specific times set for certain activities. Another method to use for staying on track with a routine is by following a sequence and not using time limitations. Proceed with activities in order rather than according to a specific time frame. For example, at night you may always read a story *after* bath time. This sequence of activities may occur at 7 or 8 pm, but it will always happen in the same order.

Opportunities for self-expression

We all need some time to unwind, whether we are three years old or 93. Let the child know that you understand his need to flap or stare at the dust particles in the light coming through the windows. You do not always want to prevent him from doing something he enjoys. It is important, however, for the child to learn that there is a time and a place for everything.

It is important to teach children to engage in enjoyable behaviors in a safe and appropriate setting. Permitting and providing an opportunity for the child to engage in these behaviors when he chooses, in the privacy of his own room, is helpful. You might consider allowing him some time alone in the family vehicle before he enters school, or a relative's house, for example.

Self-calming materials and furniture

A favorite chair or space can turn an ordinary room into a sanctuary for a child with ASD. Perhaps the child has a favorite blanket or a piece of a blanket that he carries around. This object allows the child to feel safe and is familiar and comforting to him no matter where he is or what he is doing. If the child has such an object, allow him to keep it—by using this object as a self-calming tool, he is learning the important skill of taking care of himself.

One calming technique will not work all the time or in every situation for the child. Paying attention to the specific requirements of each situation will be a great help to your child as you both continue on the learning journey.

At times an appropriate piece of furniture can be very calming. A bean bag chair is an example. When the child sits in a soft bean bag chair and it surrounds him with cushioning, he may feel like he is getting a great big hug around his entire body. This deep pressure feeling can be soothing. Perhaps you might schedule his reading time each day in such a chair. He will feel calm and more able to concentrate on the pictures and words in his books. Teaching the child to feel calm will provide him with a wonderful tool. The more he is able to control his stress and anxieties, the more able he will be to get through difficult situations successfully.

Perhaps the child always seems to be moving or touching the walls, individuals, or others' belongings. There are many seat cushions available for just this child, which are inflatable and textured. The child can touch and feel them as his body responds to the need to change his posture so he can remain seated. If this is just what the child needs, then his sitting at the dinner table and in school may improve!

Some textures can feel good while others result in strong and negative reactions. Many natural fibers are often more soothing than synthetic cloth—they allow air to filter in and out and usually feel cooler. As you become the expert on the child, you will learn the sort of fibers and cloth that the child enjoys. If his clothing is made of the variety of cloth he enjoys then, by all means, choose those materials when there is such a choice. Starting the child off on his day in clothing that feels calming is a good idea.

Staying calm in school

As the child enters school his opportunities to practice his skills in keeping calm will increase. School provides many more unexpected situations each day that are fairly predictable for adults. It is a good idea to speak with the child's teacher before the first day of school and explain some of the special needs of the child.

Teachers want their classes to be calm and organized. Many calming activities that help the child will help all of his classmates as well. A talented teacher takes advantage of some of these recommendations and uses them with all of her students. This is a good opportunity for the child to get what he needs without being singled out.

Here are a few ideas that have worked in many classrooms with children of all ages. The teacher and aides in the class should participate in these activities along with the children, so they are communicating their interest and enthusiasm.

1. Use movement activities during transitions. When it is time to put away the coloring and take out a book, for instance, stop for one minute. Have the students stand and reach as high as they can, all the way to the sky. As they are reaching, have the students take a big breath. Then have them lower their hands all the way to the ground and blow out all the air they have inside. Do a slow count to five for each inhale and exhale. Next have the students return to their seats and they will be ready for the next lesson. This can be repeated three or four times until all the students are bending and stretching together.

2. Simple deep breathing is always a good way for the child to feel calm. Using cues such as "smell the flowers" or "blow out the candles" make sense to the child. These are common ideas that he can relate to.

3. "Give yourself a big hug." All children need to love themselves. When things are tense is a great time to hold yourself tight and squeeze! Have the child wrap his arms around his shoulders, squeeze tight, and have him say to himself (or out loud if a group is doing this), "I am wonderful!" The child will benefit from the deep pressure and the positive message.

4. Wall push-ups are terrific for the class to do when returning from an activity that takes them out of the room. The teacher has all the children line up and face the wall. Have the children stand a foot or so (about 30 cm) away from the wall. Allow the children to push on the wall as hard as they can for a count of ten. Their arms may or may not bend. Their feet should be strongly planted and not move. Repeat this three times. They will be tired and quiet as they return to the class.

5. The child might need some exercise throughout the day. He might prefer some movements to do when he is seated and the class is involved in deskwork. During those times, the child can remain seated and reach his hands under his chair. Then the child should pull up as hard as he can. He can do this about three to five times or as many times as he needs to feel calm. He can also push down with his hands or his feet.

6. Attach a resistance band around the bottom of the child's chair to get some calming exercise while the child is sitting in his seat. The child pulls the band with his feet as he is seated. If a resistance band is not available, the child can simply wrap his feet around the legs of the chair and squeeze his legs together. The chair should *not* tip over; all four legs are to remain on the floor.

Feeling comfortable sitting at a desk on a chair may be a challenge for any child. It is important that school furniture be the correct size for the child. This will eliminate some of the difficulty with sitting still. The child should be able to sit on the chair and have his feet flat on the floor with his knees bent at a 90-degree angle.

The desk should be low enough so that the child can comfortably reach the top to write, with his shoulders relaxed and his elbows bent at a 90-degree angle. If the child is sitting with his feet swinging because he cannot reach the floor, then the desk and chair are too big. If furniture of the correct size is not available, using a sturdy box for the child to rest his feet flat or other adaptations are good ideas.

Visual schedules

By now you have found that using pictures helps the child understand the order of his day. The same is true in school. Even if the child is verbal and speaks and answers when spoken to, children with ASDs often find it easier to understand communication when a picture or written words are used to communicate the message. Teachers can simply write directions quickly on a white board for the child to follow.

Using a visual schedule is especially important in school. The child has so many things to learn, to get used to, and to respond to.

Explain to the child's teacher that using pictures or written words along with spoken words will give the child more than one way to understand what is expected of him. It will provide that all-important predictability that helps the child feel safe and calm. Some children do well when they have their own individual visual schedule on their desk. This way, they can look at their desk and see what activity is coming next without having to look around the classroom or interrupt the teacher.

There are a variety of forms for a visual schedule. A popular one is to have each activity on a one-inch (2.5 cm) square. The activity is identified with a picture or a symbol and a word on the bottom. The pictures are laminated and placed in order on a page with Velcro. After each activity is completed, the picture is removed and placed in a designated "done" envelope or page. This way the pictures can be used for the next day.

Children learn using many senses

Understanding what is being taught helps the child become more interested in learning. Once he is excited about school, his enthusiasm will grow. Feeling happy allows the child to be calm and more open to learning.

Using songs and rhymes with repetition is a great way for children with ASDs to learn. You have probably noticed how the child responds to certain songs and musical sounds. These preferences can be shared with the child's teacher and used as great teaching tools.

Hands-on teaching is also a very effective method for the child. Instead of teaching math as simply a paper and pencil subject, encourage the child's teacher to allow him to use objects to represent numbers. Learning a variety of subjects in one lesson shows the child and all the others in the class how math, for example, fits into everyday life. One example occurs when the teacher reviews the calendar. She can teach about numbers, current events, weather, and so on.

Staying calm in the community

Going out in public may be an ordeal if you and the child are not prepared. Remember that the child does well with predictability. Even if you are doing something out of the ordinary, preparing the child ahead of time as much as possible is important. Tell him what he can expect. Explain to him and show him with pictures if possible what will happen during the outing. Predicting how the outing or event will go will be easy to do if you are planning something that you have done before, such as visiting family.

When preparing to experience something new, such as a school field trip, telling a story about what may happen while being out and including how to act in response is a good teaching tool. You can write a few words about each step in the activity, and the child can participate by drawing a picture for each step. This is a great way to problem solve together. For example, let's say that you are going to a puppet show. You can write about how loud it may be when the other children laugh or applaud.

Together you and the child can mindmap ideas about how to respond when it gets too loud. He can cover his ears, put in ear plugs, or pull the hood of his sweatshirt over his head. Of course, you and the child cannot possibly be prepared for everything that may happen, but having some ideas will be very helpful indeed!

The night before

Planning the night before is extremely helpful. The time it takes to lay out clothing, pack lunches, and collect other needed items without time pressure is valuable. When you plan and prepare as much as possible the night before school or any outing, it is more likely to go well. There is less possibility that you will forget something essential.

One of the important calming tools to remember when planning and preparing for an outing is what some call a "fidget." This is a small item that fits in the child's hand. This item does not make a noise or light up; it is not distracting or annoying to others. The purpose of this item is that the child can play or "fidget" with it in one or both of his hands and it helps him feel calm. It is something that allows the child to self-calm and concentrate on something else, such as a movie or the teacher in class. Some examples of "fidgets" include a textured plastic toy, a key, a small balloon filled with starch, or an eraser. Some children have one favorite item and some find different fidgets to use each day. Allow the child to hold a fidget in his hand. You will know if this is an effective calming item for the child if he holds it and moves it around as he seems to be listening or paying attention to the world around him.

Snacks

It is difficult to remain calm when you are hungry. If the child feels uncomfortable because he is in a new situation, adding hunger to the mix is not a good idea. Bringing along a favorite and familiar snack can make the difference between a great day and a disaster. Even if the child does not need to eat the snack because he is having a great time, or is satisfied with the available food, you have a backup plan if needed.

Backpack/bag

Using the child's familiar backpack will provide some comfort for him in an unfamiliar situation. The backpack will be a familiar smell, touch, and sight. As the child wears his backpack, he is getting some calming deep pressure. This strong sensation allows him to feel calm in a new place or with new individuals. Unless wearing a backpack is totally unacceptable, if the child expresses the desire to wear his, allow it.

Clothing

What we wear can be calming or have the opposite effect. If you look at your own clothing preferences, you may notice that you have some items that you wear more than others. Perhaps you have a certain top that you wear when you want to feel especially comfortable. Children with ASDs are no different. They want to feel comfortable every day. The child will let you know by his behavior and perhaps choice which clothing pieces he prefers. Unless his favorite items are totally unacceptable for the situation or the weather, allow him to wear the clothing he feels most comfortable in. Starting out in any situation while feeling comfortable helps the day proceed in a positive way.

Children with ASDs are challenged daily. Knowing how to interpret those difficult times and planning for them can help. As the child grows you will see the wonderful person he is becoming. Allow him to express his individual talents as you help him maneuver through the world. This will be the child's and your accomplishment.

Chapter 8

Building Capacity
Optimizing Care and Treatment

Support for parents, carers, and professionals

No one can do this alone. That is, helping children with ASDs is a complex and long-term process. A group of individuals is needed to ensure and track progress and to address the needs of parents, carers, and professionals.

There are times when some children with ASDs display inappropriate and at times threatening and violent behaviors. It is not uncommon for family members to be diagnosed with post-traumatic stress disorder (PTSD) from incidences that occur. In some instances law enforcement or emergency medical care personnel need to be called into the home. At other times, children may need to be removed from the home to a hospitalization setting for the safety of the child and the family. It is important that the family and others who care for the child are provided with the support that is needed when it is needed.

The grief process

Parents of children with disabilities often experience a sense of grief. Siblings, family, and even close neighbors may feel this way as well. Often, these feelings come from a sense of loss. This could be from the realization that their child will require more assistance in their development than typical children.

Parents often worry that their child will not reach the milestones that typical children meet. Some examples of the goals that concern parents and carers are: success in school and success in life after school, having friends, and establishing other healthy relationships. These concerns generate powerful feelings that often result in strong emotions expressed to friends, family, and professionals who interact with the child. Sometimes parents feel angry and believe that the school, or agency, or someone else, can or should "fix" their child. When immediate and obvious gains are not made, these feelings often become stronger.

At times parents lose sight of their intentions and priorities. When parents are questioned they will state that what they really want is the best treatment for their children so that they can reach their highest potential. Parents may become frustrated and feel powerless when they perceive slow or no progress towards their goals. It is during these times of frustration that they demand action. Sometimes parents vent this anger by bringing litigation to agencies or schools.

Professionals often bear the brunt of these expressions of anger, and can become upset or confused when they are blamed for the child's difficulties. It is important for all involved to remember the steps in the grief process. Helping the family through the acceptance process of the diagnosis is as important as any other treatment for the child with an ASD.

This acceptance is not a linear process, however, and some steps are repeated over and over. With some individuals, the grief process never feels like it will end. Some get "stuck" and do not move forward. A skilled therapeutic professional can help and should be recommended.

Dr Elisabeth Kubler-Ross (1997) named the stages in the grief process:

1. Denial: This feeling is often expressed by parents not wanting to hear reports and diagnoses from professionals. Sometimes parents will ask for additional testing to "prove" the child does not have an ASD.

2. Anger: This is expressed often by parents blaming God, blaming individuals, or blaming agencies for their child's difficulties. Sometimes parents blame themselves and ask, "What did I do to deserve this?" or "Did I do something wrong during the pregnancy to create this?"

3. Bargaining: "If only" is an often heard term from parents. "If only my child receives [example service or treatment], she will be completely fine." Parents want a way out of the situation, and think of ways to make reality change to meet their emotional needs.

4. Depression: Sadness and despair can be seen even in the body language of some parents of children with ASDs. Feelings of helplessness and loss of hope for the future are expressed in many ways.

5. Acceptance: The hope is that parents come to terms with the situation. In this way they may better lead positive, fulfilling lives with their child with an ASD.

Friends, family, and professionals can certainly help provide support to each other during this grieving process. It is suggested that information about the grief process is shared so that all involved know that there is an end to such suffering.

Networking and a team approach

It is highly suggested for parents, carers, and professionals to develop a network or team of individuals to provide technical, hands-on, and general support to assist in the care and development of any child with an ASD. Working together in such a fashion is often termed a multi-disciplinary team. This team approach is valuable because new information and research findings are reported in the professional literature before that information is available to the general public.

Each professional is ethically bound to keep up-to-date with the latest research in their particular field. They are often aware of new techniques for treatment before those treatments become part of the more popular culture. The more talented professionals will identify new treatments as soon as they are reported, and use them if and when they are appropriate.

Many research studies are currently underway regarding ASDs. Trial and error is often part of finding ways to help on an individualized basis. Using this somewhat experimental approach requires the careful input of many qualified and caring team members.

Who should be part of this network or team? Of course, parents, carers, and professionals need to be part of the team, but also consider the child who has the ASD. A child as young as three years old or even younger is able to express ideas. Those ideas can lead to very creative and individualized treatments when they are used by the adults involved. Keeping the child as actively involved as possible in the process of his growth and development will set the stage for keeping him active in his progress. This is a good lesson for him to learn, as an important goal is that he becomes as responsible for his own success as possible.

Note that no one person on the team has the "answer" no matter how many degrees and how much experience they may have. The following are just some of the professionals and service providers who may be part of such a team. They are listed in no particular order. These professionals work closely with the occupational therapist as part of the team. As we have expressed in previous chapters, the occupational therapist focuses on functional skills and abilities to help children develop. For the young child, the role he has is primarily that of a child, and the role of student, sibling, and friend.

Types of professionals and services
PSYCHIATRISTS

While there is no known cause or treatment for ASDs, physicians or psychiatrists specializing in children with ASDs are often a critical part of the treatment team. They can also provide information about treatment modalities and suggestions for families and the team. Perhaps most important is providing medication management for children with ASDs.

Medication management is a complex process. While any physician can prescribe medication, a psychiatrist or physician who specializes in ASDs can determine a course of medication, over time, that best suits an individual. Medications are tolerated differently, even with children with the same diagnoses in the same family. Medication management can often be a difficult process for families, carers, and professionals because children may have negative reactions to some medications.

Some medications cause increased anxiety or significant weight gain, while others have no effect. It is important for families and team members to communicate the effects of new medications or new combinations of medicines to the treating psychiatrist or physician. As children age, medications may need to be adjusted due to this factor as well. As a child grows, gains weight, and develops, he will respond differently to his medication.

PSYCHOLOGISTS

Psychologists provide diagnostic information but also specific recommendations about planning and implementing treatment for children with ASDs. Depending on where you live, different credentials are required for the provision of a diagnosis. It is important that the professional making the initial diagnosis has the correct credentials to do so, as this may have an impact on insurance and the opportunity for treatment eligibility. Required eligibility information is available from state agencies or insurance providers where relevant.

Psychologists can help develop behavioral plans that address a myriad of needs. Behavioral plans work best when all involved follow the plan consistently. This communicates a stable message to the child and increases the chance that he will generalize new skills. Generalization is another goal that demonstrates that something the child has learned has carried over to more than one place. For example, if the child has learned good table manners at home, he will use those manners at school and at a friend's home as well.

Psychologists can also provide information about adapting the home, classroom, or other settings to help ensure success of the child. They can also provide emotional support needed for families who may be under a great deal of stress. Psychologists can be a resource to help the family develop a support system, by encouraging them to identify community groups, friends, and family members to call upon when they are in need.

GENERAL EDUCATION TEACHERS

General education teachers absolutely need to be part of the team. They often do not have the specialized knowledge that other members of the team have regarding ASDs. They will benefit from knowing what works and what does not when it comes to learning, development, and behaviors. Parents and the school-based professionals are often called upon to help the general education teacher with providing the best education for the child. This information is presented in relation to the accommodations that work best for the individual child.

SPECIAL EDUCATION TEACHERS

Special education teachers often have an understanding of the unique learning needs of children with various disabilities. They also often need information about specifically addressing learning, development, and behavioral needs. They typically provide support if not direct intervention relating to specific objectives noted on individualized education plans. Open and frequent communication between all the professionals in the school system ensures the most consistent and highest standards for the treatment of the child.

PARAEDUCATORS

Paraeducators are also referred to as classroom or individual aides or paraprofessionals. They often provide the individual child with support throughout the day at school to ensure success. It is recommended that they receive training so they understand some basics about ASD. This book is a good way to provide that information.

Paraeducators should be encouraged to attend treatment and individualized education program meetings. During these meetings they will learn about the specific goals for the child and professional evaluation results. It is important that all who work with the child have the knowledge and skills to address his needs.

SPEECH THERAPISTS

Language development difficulties are often shown in children with ASDs. In fact, siblings of children with ASDs have a higher incidence of language difficulties. Speech therapists provide a whole host of services including advice and consultation, assessment, one-to-one intervention, or group language therapies. Speech therapists who work for schools typically focus on helping the child access the curriculum by providing interventions to prevent language difficulties from impairing progress in the curriculum. Non-school therapists can provide services to help remedy speech and language issues.

Children with ASDs often need assistance learning about pragmatic language skills. These skills include learning how to interpret idioms, slang, sayings, and social situations. Playing appropriately, asking for help, and using appropriate language in social situations are all part of pragmatic language. Speech therapists and occupational therapists often work together on social competency skill programs.

PHYSICAL THERAPISTS

Similar to occupational therapists, physical therapists address movement as it relates to functioning in the world. Gross or large motor concerns are the specialty of physical therapists. However, both occupational and physical therapists are concerned with sensory, balance, coordination, and the learning needs of children with ASDs. Physical therapists assess a number of developmental issues by examining muscular, neuromuscular, and other body systems.

Physical therapists can develop and implement exercise activities and sensory diets and interventions. These can help children deal with anxiety and encourage calmness in addition to other physical benefits.

FAMILY THERAPISTS

Families with children with disabilities have a higher rate of divorce than average. There is no doubt that having a child with an ASD provides an array of stress, confusion, and added work to any family. Having such a child can bring out the very best, but at times the very worst in relationship patterns. This is true for both the relationship between parents with siblings, and the child with an ASD as well.

Family therapists can provide support, information, and encouragement to help families make it through tough times. Difficult times may last months to years. Just learning of the diagnosis can be traumatic. The intense feelings of fear, anxiety, and sense of loss is at first often greater than the reality of the situation. A family therapist can help families see the true picture of what is happening. This therapist can help the family move beyond the emotions of the moment.

IN-HOME PROVIDERS

Providers of in-home care come in a broad array of services—family treatment professionals, behavior aides for the child, and health care aides. Services may be direct to the child and combine consultation or emotional supports for the family.

BEHAVIOR THERAPISTS

Behavior therapists, also known as behavior specialists, etc., provide direct and consultative support to the entire team. They help to develop behavioral assessments and interventions. Additionally, they can provide techniques for children with ASDs and families to help deal with the stresses and strains of daily life. For example, behavior therapists educate the family and others about cognitive techniques that provide tools for coping with negative and ongoing events.

Many of the professionals listed above provide a variety of services. For example, psychologists can provide family therapy. In-home providers often consist of psychologists or counselors who specialize in family therapy. It is important for the team to develop a plan that can be understood by all members of the team and that is carried out consistently.

Assessment and goal planning

Appropriate programming starts with as complete an evaluation as possible. It is important that the evaluation indicates the exact areas of strength and needs for children with ASDs. Identifying problem areas can then help all involved efficiently and effectively to direct their energies. Additionally, specifying problem areas in detail is important for progress monitoring and to ensure overall developmental gains. Fortunately, there are a number of assessments that are available.

The Introduction explains those assessments specific to occupational therapy. Here are some additional assessments that do not provide a diagnosis, although they do provide detailed information about strengths and needs. Such information can then be used to develop a robust treatment plan. It is important that any treatment plan has specific goals and objectives that may be measured often. In this way, changes to treatment may be made depending on the success or lack of success for any given intervention.

1. Assessment of Basic Language and Learning Skills—Revised (ABLLS) (Partington 2006; Patten-Koenig and Rudney 2010; Polatajko and Cantin 2010): This assessment is for children aged three to nine. It includes not just an assessment but also an individualized education development guide.

2. Functional Behavioral Assessments: Such assessments take into consideration those factors that lead up to problem behaviors, what those specific behaviors are, and the responses needed to address them. Functional Behavioral Assessments require observations by more than one person and across different settings. Team members look at the behavior information to further describe the assessment, behaviors, and behavior intervention planning. Such an assessment does not need to be purchased, although several companies market information and related documents.

3. PsychoEducational Profile Revised (PEP-R) (Schopler *et al.* 1990; Segal 1998, 2000, 2004; Segal and Beyer 2006; Segal and Frank 1998; Segal and Hinojosa 2006): This assessment also provides program planning information. It is designed for children aged six months to seven years. Development information relating to fine and gross motor, perception, and eye–hand coordination is assessed. Behavioral information is also addressed as well as cognition, play, language, and sensory areas.

4. BRIGANCE® Comprehensive Inventory of Basic Skills II (Glascoe 2010; Grandin 2008; Hinojosa and Blount 2004): This assessment is designed for children aged 5 through to 13. Academic and developmental skills are addressed. Information for program planning is also given.

Celebration

Children with ASDs make a great deal of progress, but often not as quickly as their peers. It is important that you take the time to cherish those small and large areas in which growth is seen. Not only will this encourage the child, but parents, carers, and professionals as well.

References

Autism Speaks (2011) 'What is autism?' Available at www.autismspeaks.org/what-autism, accessed on 30 September 2011.

Glascoe, F. (2010) *BRIGANCE® Comprehensive Inventory of Basic Skills-II (CIBS-R)*. North Billerica, MA: Curriculum Associates, Inc.

Grandin, T. (2008) *The Way I See It: A Personal Look at Autism and Asperger's*. Arlington, TX: Future Horizons, Inc.

Hinojosa, J. and Blount, M.-L. (2004) "Purposeful Activities Within the Context of Occupational Therapy." In J. Hinojosa and M.-L. Blount (eds) *The Texture of Life: Purposeful Activities in Occupational Therapy* (2nd edition). Bethesda, MD: American Occupational Therapy Association.

Kubler-Ross, E. (1997) *On Death and Dying*. Beaverton, OR: Touchstone.

Kuhaneck, M. and Watling, R. (2010) *Autism: A Comprehensive Occupational Therapy Approach* (3rd edition). Bethesda, MD: AOTA Press.

Lieberman, D. and Scheer, J. (2002) "Evidence-based practice forum: AOTA's evidence-based literature review project: An overview." *American Journal of Occupational Therapy 56*, 3, 344–349.

Partington, J. (2006) *Assessment of Basic Language and Learning Skills—Revised*. Los Angeles, CA: Western Psychological Services.

Patten-Koenig, K. and Rudney, S.G. (2010) "Performance challenges for children and adolescents with difficulty processing and integrating sensory information: A systematic review." *American Journal of Occupational Therapy 64*, 3, 430–442.

Polatajko, H. and Cantin, N. (2010) "Exploring the effectiveness of occupational therapy interventions, other than the sensory integration approach, with children and adolescents experiencing difficulty processing and integrating sensory information." *American Journal of Occupational Therapy 64*, 3, 415–429.

Schopler, E., Reichler, R.J., Bashford, A., Lansing, M.D. and Marcus, L.M. (1990) *The Psychoeducational Profile Revised*. Austin, TX: Pro-Ed.

Segal, R. (1998) "The construction of family occupations: A study of families with children who have attention deficit/hyperactivity disorder." *Canadian Journal of Occupational Therapy 65*, 286–292.

Segal, R. (2000) "Adaptive strategies of mothers with children with attention deficit hyperactivity disorder: Enfolding and unfolding occupations." *American Journal of Occupational Therapy 54*, 300–306.

Segal, R. (2004) "Family routines and rituals: A context for occupational therapy interventions." *American Journal of Occupational Therapy 58*, 499–508.

Segal, R. and Beyer, C. (2006) "Integration and application of a home treatment program: A study of parents and occupational therapists." *American Journal of Occupational Therapy 60*, 500–510.

Segal, R. and Frank, G. (1998) "The extraordinary construction of ordinary experience: Scheduling daily life in families with children with attention deficit hyperactivity disorder." *Scandinavian Journal of Occupational Therapy 5*, 141–147.

Segal, R. and Hinojosa, J. (2006) "The activity setting of homework: An analysis of three cases and implications for occupational therapy." *American Journal of Occupational Therapy 60*, 50–59.

Zwaigenbaum, L., Bryson, S., Lord, C., Rogers, S. *et al.* (2009) "Clinical assessment and management of toddlers with suspected Autism Spectrum Disorder: Insights from studies of high-risk infants." *Pediatrics 123*, 5, 1383–1391.

Index